The Path of of Femininity

The 6 Gifts of Your Sovereignty

ÉLÉONORE DE POSSON

Published by Made to Change the World Publishing
Nashville, Tennessee

Cover art by Olivia de Posson
www.oliviadeposson.com

Cover and interior design by Chelsea Jewell

ISBN: 978-1-956837-00-1 Paperback
978-1-956837-01-8 eBook

Printed in the USA, Canada and Europe

To my son Benjamin,
whose masculine energy in my womb inspired
me to write a book about feminine energy.
It's all about sacred union.

TABLE OF CONTENTS

Throughout this book are references to a workbook of exercises for you to learn about feminine and masculine energy as well as to practice deeply integrating the six gifts of your sovereignty. Please find that workbook on my website at www.eleonoredeposson.com/workbookpof.

Foreword

Hidden from view for nearly 2000 years, the Path of the Feminine has been demonized, suppressed, mocked and devalued so that destruction and war could reign supreme. And now we find ourselves situated at the peak of mayhem when it appears that humanity has never been more divided and chaotic. It is here that we stand directly in front of a portal where, when entered, we will ascend to a level of harmony, both individually and collectively, beyond our comprehension simply because our mind cannot fathom what it has not seen before.

Due to its mysterious nature, feminine energy is not something logically understood; it is an energy within us that we must understand through bodily experience. The Path of Femininity serves as an invitation to see for yourself the gifts that await your discovery. Eléonore's embodiment of the tools she offers in this book is unparalleled, and she is incredibly gifted at translating the feminine mysteries into accessible, practical applications for your life. Don't mistake her soft, sweet nature for weakness because, as you read this book, you'll receive the pillars of a New Revolution—rebellion simply through being your authentic self.

There is no coincidence that this book found its way onto your path. Return to its pages again and again, and you'll uncover more of yourself than you ever deemed possible. May you hold tight to the wisdom within its pages and birth its magnificence into your own life not only for yourself, but for generations to come.

It's time for the rise of the feminine and its union with the masculine once again. It's time for you to reclaim your sovereignty and become the master of your destiny. It is time.

-Makhosi Hefisah Nejeser, The Royal Shaman

Acknowledgments

First, I'd like to thank my dear husband, Rich. You have always believed in me and brought me back to my truth. I love that you consistently reminded me that this book was not "crazy"—just my new normal of allowing Life to work through me. Thank you for the countless hours of discussing the feminine, the masculine, sacred union and sacred sexuality. Words don't describe how much I love you.

Thank you, mon amour de Benji. The gift of my pregnancy with you brought me the creativity and intuition I needed to step into my most authentic and spiritual self. Giving birth to you in the comfort of our home made me feel more powerful than ever before. The sovereignty you gifted me from these two experiences truly allowed me to give birth to this book.

Makhosi Nejeser—thank you for your beautiful and wise Foreword. Your teachings, support and guidance help me bring all of myself into my work and life.

Lesha Nelson—thank you for your womb wisdom and for showing me that I was meant to lead a divine feminine movement. Here it is!

Deepshikha Sairam—thank you for your coaching and friendship that made me realize it was time to surrender.

Seren Bertrand—thank you for your immense knowledge and your books; they created many synchronicities in my life and made me see that I was a womb priestess.

Kaia Ra—thank you for the *Sophia Code*, which (re)connected me to Mary Magdalene. I've felt her with me since I read it. She helped me write this book.

Sahara Rose—thank you for reminding me I was a Teacher and for helping me embrace that archetype.

Paula Hartley—thank you for bringing Benjamin to Life with me. I have been so blessed to have you as a midwife. Your expertise and friendship were key to experiencing the limitless power of a woman.

Ellie Shefi and her team—thank you for guiding the publication of this book so that it could end up in my readers' hands.

I would also like to thank Glennon Doyle, Anita Moorjani, Tosha Silver, Michael Singer, Allan Lokos, Marianne Williamson and Arouna Lipschitz, whose works have taught me a lot. I had to quote their wisdom in these pages. And thanks to Deva Premal— your music inspired me and helped me connect to my truth during the creative writing process of this book.

Introduction

It's 4:00 am. I'm in a hotel for a romantic getaway with my husband. I wake up from a dream that feels very real. In it, I witnessed a friend dressed like a priestess, wearing a golden and white gown, surrounded by a flower arch, sitting on a chair while I sat on the floor listening to her. She talked to me and delivered a very clear message. I know that when we remember our dreams so precisely, it means our guides are communicating with us. So, I get up, grab my phone and write the message in my notes app. The message says: "The version of you that smiles, does what is expected of her and hides her originality will not work anymore. 2021 is a year of change for you. We are asking you to show up with authenticity."

As I write this, I receive more information about what authenticity means. I transcribe what I hear, excited and amazed by what I'm discovering. Then I put my phone back down on the night table and lay my head on the pillow. I try to fall asleep, but another download arrives. More information is given to me. I can feel it's coming from outside of me and is something I have never thought of before. It is a very curious experience. My mind is completely awake and super active, similar to experiencing a kundalini awakening. I grab my phone again and write everything that I can understand, hear and feel. The information is given to me in a fraction of a second, yet holds a 10-minute speech. It's like receiving information with different dimensions and trying to transcribe it into a linear language. Tricky but thrilling. Suddenly, the title and subtitle of this book are given to me. I'm amazed! I can't believe what's happening. I don't try to understand it either; I'm just in the moment. Then I ask: "I'm confused, what six gifts are you talking about?" I hear: "We are sharing four gifts with you today; you already know the others." Alright. I am really learning a lesson, in the middle of the night, taught by invisible, very wise and bright energies.

In this hotel room, with my husband sleeping next to me, I learn that authenticity, magnetism, intuition, surrender, receiving and grounding are keys to being the sovereigns of our lives. And that it is important to act from that place of "power" to become channels of Life. This teaching is mandatory for the evolution of Humanity and needs to be understood by many so that we can all allow Life, Source, the Universe—whatever you want to call it—to operate through us, for our highest good and the highest good of others. It is healing for our divine feminine energy and will allow a new age to take place. I also learn that a daily practice of physical, emotional, mental and spiritual self-care is necessary to stay in that place of sovereignty and be the true creators that we were always meant to be. I'm blown away. I feel so close to truth. Yet my words poorly describe my feelings. Actually, I feel like I'm experiencing truth itself. A deep truth I intuitively always knew has just been spoken to me. I suddenly think, "The world has no idea. We have no idea. I have no idea. I know nothing and there is so much to learn." My body vibrates from excitement and evidence. Everything makes so much sense.

After an hour of receiving and writing, I ask them to stop and to come back another day. The session was intense physically. Because we live in human bodies and they don't, we need to set loving boundaries with light beings. I then *see* two doors closing on each other and feel my forehead, my third eye, closing. Then… silence. They're gone. I'm writing "they" but have no idea how many there were. Four, five perhaps? One did most of the talking but I could feel others too. The silence fills the room, and my body takes some time to integrate it all. I feel huge waves of energy going through my upper body. I'm dizzy. The whole room is turning. It's like being on a boat in a storm. As an energy healer, I know all I need to do is to surrender and ground myself. It will pass. I breathe, drink some water and visualize roots around my feet. A few minutes later, it slows down. I'm cold, which is normal after receiving the energy update that comes with these teachings. I put on a jumper and fall asleep. Exhausted. Excited but exhausted.

These teachings are the foundation for the rising of the divine feminine. Part 1 of this book lays the basics of feminine and masculine energy. Understanding this will create a strong basis for you to integrate Part 2. Part 1 covers:

- Feminine and masculine energies.
- When you act with each of them.
- How they impact your life differently.
- When you are wounded or healed.
- How you can heal the wounded feminine.

Part 2 addresses the core teachings I received that night and during the next months. It covers:

- The six gifts of sovereignty.
- How you can unlock them within yourself.
- How they lead you to become the sovereign of your own life.
- Why it is so important to step up as the sovereign of your life, now.

This teaching is part of my life's work, and I cannot emphasize enough how important it is. Today, more than ever, we really need this. If you're holding this book in your hands, it is because you have been called to integrate this work into your life. You have answered the call of your soul which signed up to be part of the change. You are the change—the great change of Humanity allowing us to move into a Golden Age. An age where we are all sovereigns, connected to our inner power, sharing our unique gifts with the world and co-creators of Life.

I have done my very best to leave the teachings as intact and pure as possible. But as with every channeled message, use your own discernment and intuition to take what resonates and leave what doesn't. It is inevitable that my own personality and experiences filter and express the teachings in a certain way that could be slightly different from what was meant to come through. So please, start with being sovereign today and read this book through the filter of your own intelligence, intuition, experience and heart.

This book is not for everybody, but if you're still reading, it is definitely for you. And I could not be more thrilled to embark on this journey with you. We are the change we have been waiting for.

Part 1

Feminine and Masculine Energy

Chapter 1

The Rise of Sacred Feminine Energy: Why Now?

Yesterday

When did we stop trusting our feminine, intuitive, sensual, embodied energy?

When did women become a threat?

Why are we suddenly talking so much about feminine energy?

These questions find their answers back in history. His-story. Like author Lisa Lister points out, we talk about his story, not her story. The past has been written by men, and most often from the side of the victorious. Women did not get much of a say in history. Still, reading through the lines of the story written by men, we can find answers. I would like to start in 325 A.D. at the Council of Nicaea. This Council was the first general Council in the history of the Roman Catholic Church. It was a response to all different, conflicting and troubling teachings considered dangerous to the salvation of souls that were being spread around the Mediterranean Sea. The Council gathered Christian bishops to debate the divine nature of Jesus, establish uniform dates for Easter and create a set of laws, called the Canon Law, to regulate the ecclesiastic authority. The doctrine was created. The Church became an authority. *The* authority.

Either during the Council or soon thereafter, the Church also chose which texts would constitute the Bible. Though sacred text, the Bible was also created as propaganda, a tool to establish the authority of the Church and Christianism. Any included text had to have the power to inform and to convert. Anything that didn't suit this purpose was intentionally left aside. Like women. The Bible talks about Mother Mary and Mary Magdalene, but it limits their roles to a virgin mother and a whore. We know little about these two women. They are described through their sexuality, which is either absent or dirty. The Gospels don't reveal if they were healers, leaders, great cooks or had any other gifts. Let's take a closer look at what the word virgin, *ver-gin*, actually means. Today's definition of "virgin" is a pure, untouched woman who hasn't yet experienced penetration. But before Jesus was even born, the old Latin word, "ver-gin" meant something completely different. It described an independent, untied, sovereign woman. A woman in her own power. Her own lover. Isis, Hathor and other goddesses were all called "ver-gins." Mother Mary was a ver-gin, for sure, but definitely not a virgin the way we hear it today.

Mary Magdalene was known to be sexual. She was in her senses, in her body, in her creativity, in her intuition and in her power, and that was scary for men. They made sure it was a shameful, dirty place to be in by changing the understanding of sexual to shameful. Like they changed the definition of virgin from powerful to untouched. Why limit these women to their sexuality? Why even change their sexuality to something absent or dirty? They must have been very potent for men to want to limit their presence and place in His-story. I believe that Mary Magdalene's presence and power was a struggle for the Church because she was Jesus' rock. The Bible says they met at the wedding at Cana, where Jesus changed water into wine. Some believe that the Bible omits that it was actually their wedding. More and more channeled books talk about the critical role Mary Magdalene played in Jesus' life. *The Sophia Code, Magdalene Mysteries, The Forbidden Female Speaks, The Magdalen Manuscript* and *Womb Awakening* all share a very similar story: Mary Magdalene was Jesus' partner and she helped him tremendously in his task because she was initiated to do so. I'm not trying to rewrite the truth or hoping to convince you. Just consider that she might have been much more important than what we were led to believe. In Her-story, she was probably a healer, like him. She was a psychic, like him. She had a direct connection to Source, like him. She served him, so that he could serve the world. She helped him reach enlightenment so that he could go through the death initiation and resurrection. She was called a whore because she was initiated to sacred sexual practices. Perhaps it was these practices that helped Jesus on an alchemical level to step into being the leader and healer we know him as. It is because of the power she had—the power she gave him— that she inherited the title "whore." Her power, knowledge and embodiment became a source of shame. Magdalene was in her power and got rejected by the Church for it. I believe that they left her to the side, giving her a tiny, insignificant role to make sure that other women would not be inspired. That way, the authority of the Church would not be challenged. This version of history has deeply, deeply impacted our society.

For centuries, women in their power were shamed for it, whether they were in their sexual power, sharing their gifts with the world or making money. Being in their power came with backlash, criticism, shame and rejection. The same way Magdalene's power was rejected by the Church and made dirty, our natural intuition, creative power, inner wisdom, emotions and surrendered state became a source of shame and rejection. Women were led to believe they had to give life and nothing more. All that creative, intuitive power was reduced to motherhood only so that the authority of men was not shaken. It worked for about 2000–3000 years. But then His-story began to be slowly disrupted by women who knew they were more than baby-making machines and started reclaiming their power.

Fast forward a few centuries to 1918. That's the year women received the right to vote for the first time. It happened in the UK. The US followed in 1920; it took another 22 years to see French women vote. The last countries to grant that right to women were Oman, Kuwait and Afghanistan in the early 2000s. It's barely been 100 years since women first received the right to vote, the right to be heard. Just writing these words makes my mind go crazy. How has keeping women silent for so long even been possible?

Another important date in the story of the feminine is 1951. That's the year the UK repealed the Witchcraft Act. This law, which passed in 1735, allowed the hunting and execution of witches. And by witches, it meant healers, herbalists, medicine women, midwives, mediums. Every intuitive woman who shared her gifts with the world. Every woman in her power. That power would scare the Church, the military, the politicians and probably the businessmen as well. The whole society basically. Helen Duncan is considered the last woman to have been convicted under the Witchcraft Act. She supposedly contacted the spirit of a sailor of the HMS Barham, a boat who's sinking had been hidden from the public at the time. The military feared that she would reveal the secret plans for D-Day, the Normandy Landing of June 6, 1944, which ended World War II. She spent nine months in jail. The Witchcraft Act of 1735 inspired other countries. The Witchcraft Suppression Act of 1957 in South Africa was in place until 2016. The physical hunting of women in their power has almost disappeared today. But it has been replaced by a more subtle, psychological hunting created by social and cultural pressure, the need to fit in and the silent rules of patriarchy.

For centuries, we have been suppressed, tortured, burned, killed. Controlled by fear and the patriarchal society in place, we did our best to stay small. When I use the term "patriarchal society," I do not mean men only. Even though it has very strong masculine values of competition, strength and effectiveness, women were also responsible for its rise. We played a role in the diminishing game. We followed the rules without question and helped the authority in place by reporting women who wouldn't respect those rules. This created a huge and still prevalent mistrust among women: the sisterhood wound. So many sisters competing with each other. So many mothers not getting along with their daughters. The past centuries have created generations of women feeling unworthy, unheard, unseen, unloved—wounded by a patriarchal society to which they contributed. The time for change is now.

Today

In the last century, and especially the last 50 years, things started changing faster. Women received a seat around the table. We got the right to talk, vote and work. We were finally heard. With shaking hands but determination, we took our shot and adapted to the masculine society in place. We tried to fit in by hiding our differences as much as possible while behaving, as much as we could, like men. We started working like them. Wearing pants, like them. Competing, like them. Setting goals and pushing, like them. Going back to work three weeks after giving birth, like them. We wanted so badly to keep our place in life outside home that we did everything like them. We never thought we could do it our own way. We bent to the secret rules in place. And while still being women, we juggled the impossible: be a whore in bed but a saint in the kitchen; be smart but don't outshine your husband; be sensitive but not too emotional; be beautiful but not too sexy; be focused but not too ambitious; etc. *Be* but *don't be too much.* It's a modern torture we have been imposing on ourselves for decades and are still imposing on ourselves today, one driven by the fear of not fitting in and being rejected again.

It is so exhausting that we release the pressure by criticizing other women if they don't fit in that very, very narrow definition of "How to be a woman." We judge the girl who's wearing too much makeup, attracting too much attention, launching her business, saying something inappropriate, making lots of money or being flirty, lazy, funny, crazy, stupid, bossy. We criticize the woman that does not fit into this set of rules because we believe we have to. That's how deep our patriarchal/masculine society still runs in 2021. And deep down, we are so tired of it.

We're struggling.

Seeing another woman that seems to have it all—the purposeful business, the loving husband, the flat tummy, the handsome kids, the dream home with the infinity pool—is hard to face when we're trying to follow the rules and feel like we're getting nowhere. It's like admitting we've been playing a game that's supposed to be fun, but we haven't been enjoying it since the beginning. The game is not fun. But we stick to the rules in place. We hang on. Because that's what most women do, right? And some say they love it and are really enjoying it! So, we must be the problem. Maybe we didn't understand the whole game and the fun is yet to come? We want to believe so. We stay in the game. We keep doing, giving, setting goals, pushing to reach them, protecting, showing confidence and hoping that one day, maybe the fun that's been promised will show up.

Nope.

It will never show up because we have been playing the game with the wrong rules; that's why it's not fun for us. That's why it's not working. That's why we're exhausted, burned out, overeating, over-giving…. We're tired of pushing, tired of feeling like a failure, tired of feeling like something is off.

Wait a second. You also feel like something is off? You feel like something is not working? You feel *something*, right? Amazing! Because feeling is your joker. It will help you set up the rules with which you should be playing the game of life. Yes, you can create your own rules for your own life! And feeling what's right or not for you is what will help you define these rules. It's easy for you to feel, right? I know, you feel so much! You feel everything. What if that is actually your superpower? What if your emotions are your superpower? What if you aren't too emotional, but too gifted? What if you only have to follow your emotions and go where they guide you to? That would be easy for you, right? Who said the game of life was supposed to be hard?

Tomorrow

The key to set your own rules and experience a life of ease, purpose and abundance is to reconnect with your feminine energy. Feminine energy is power, creation, connection and flow. When you let your feminine lead the way and allow your masculine energy to serve her, ease and flow become your new normal. There's no hustling, worrying or controlling necessary. Your emotions and intuition guide and support you. They show you what you need, where to go, what suits you and what doesn't. You thought the opposite, right? I know, we have all been led to believe that emotions are "bad." But it is time to give them back their nobility. It's time for you to take back your power. This power also connects you with your intuition. This inner wisdom is meant to help you move forward and make the right choices. It is a compass that leads you to your creative power so that you can birth projects, ideas, and bring Life on Earth in all its forms. Because at your core, you are a creatrix. A woman who is deeply connected to herself and the feminine source of creative power.

The time to heal and awaken your divine feminine energy is now. Witness your life change, align and bring you more than you could have imagined, instead of living a life dictated by old-fashioned rules created by men who feared your power.

Chapter 2

Feminine and Masculine Energy

A World of Energies

You are pure energy. Energy in constant movement. Ancient eastern wisdoms have been teaching this for a very long time. Traditional Chinese medicine and yogic wisdom present these as yin and yang energies, the feminine and the masculine. These two aspects of energy respond to and balance each other perpetually, in everything and every being. You could consider them opposites, but they are interdependent. They need each other to live; the night is yin, the day is yang, but there's no day without night. You too are made of both energies that need to circulate freely to be healthy physically, emotionally, mentally and spiritually.

Yin energy is feminine energy. It represents matter, as this word has the same etymological root of the word "mother." It's the Earth and the crib, but also the root of the yang energy which is more volatile and immaterial. Yang energy is masculine energy. It births from the yin and needs a stable yin. If your yin, your feminine energy, is not strong enough, it can't keep the volatile, masculine, active energy grounded. Instead, this hot, pushy energy will take over and burn you out. I love how there's a lot of hidden wisdom in the words we use every day. The well-known term "burnout" literally means that our masculine, warm energy burns us from the inside out. This energy is all about doing, pushing and executing, and can very much exhaust us. Our society is mostly yang. Masculine values such as action, competition, performance or speed have been praised throughout past centuries, and definitely more in the last 50 years. Whereas receptivity, creativity, intuition and deliberateness have been considered weak and flaky. Without knowing it, we find ourselves desperate to invite in more yin energy because we need a strong feminine foundation to hold the volatile masculine energy.

Balancing these energies is key to prevent burn out, depression and illnesses, and, critically, to create an abundant, aligned, joyful and effortless life or business. This is true not just for women but for men as well. Men and women both need this today. Men also have feminine energy and need to stabilize this birthing, grounding, intuitive energy to allow their masculine, providing, protecting, doing energy to be at its best.

I truly believe that healing and awakening your feminine energy is what you have been waiting for. But you probably didn't even know you wanted or needed it. Or that it was a thing. Right? Well, rest assured, that's also what happened to me. A whole new world opened to me when I realized I needed to balance both energies within myself. I observed the tremendous impact it had on the exhausting lifestyle I lived. It changed my habits, my rhythm, my health, my sense of purpose, my creativity, my income. And that is what I want for you too.

By reconnecting with these two energies and knowing which one you operate from throughout your day, you can make better choices for yourself, leave your wounded and pushy ego to the side and let your intuition and inner wisdom guide you. Your yin energy craves attention and wants to be put on a pedestal again to bring you back into balance, and offer health, abundance and joy in your life, and also in your business and relationships. These are the gifts she has been waiting to give you. Are you ready to harvest them?

Opening Yourself to Feminine and Masculine Energies

Download your **workbook** (available at www.eleonoredeposson. com/workbookpof) and refer to Exercise 1 to do the following exercise completely. It will invite you to look at the two lists below and answer further questions.

Giving	Receiving
Protecting	Surrendering
Providing	Creating
Competing	Deciding on intuition
Logical thinking	Being spontaneous
Discipline	Slowing down
Doing	Reflecting
Goal setting	Feeling
Being structured	Being

Which list is most like you? There's no good or bad answer. We actually need a balance of these two lists in our everyday life. But my bet is that you probably identify more with the list on the left, the masculine energy. Is that correct? It's completely normal. Our Western upbringing is very masculine. Our society—companies, media, entertainment—praise these masculine values. We have been raised to perform and excel. Every day, we think, act, give, do, compete, set goals, push to reach them, sleep, repeat.

Ask yourself what percent of the time you are in your feminine energy, the list on the right. Receiving, surrendering, feeling, reflecting, grounding, etc.? Five percent, 20 percent, 50 percent of the time? Write that percent down and then repeat this exercise when you finish the book. Compare your answers. One purpose of this book is to increase your awareness about your own balance of yin and yang energy so that you can consciously invite in more feminine or masculine energy. And then observe how a new balance will deeply transform your life.

For years, I lived in my masculine energy. And I didn't know. I didn't know what it meant, what it drained, what it provoked. And I didn't know that I didn't know. I just went on with my life, making it as fun, perfect and fulfilling as I could. But it wasn't really working to be honest....

My first interaction with the notion of masculine and feminine energy was somewhere around 2011; I was 23. I was struggling with gluten and lactose intolerance and had daily stomach pains. My gut was trying to tell me something was off, but I had no clue about body-mind connection at the time. I was just annoyed by the pain and the fact that I could not eat most things I liked: bread, cheese, pasta, pizza, yoghurt, cake.... Yes, I had a poor diet and was also struggling with eating disorders at the time.

A close friend of mine told me she had seen a Traditional Chinese Medicine specialist and that she came out of the meeting with a custom list of ingredients she could and could not eat. I loved the idea of getting support to feed myself with ingredients my body would accept. I booked an appointment. Two weeks later, I visited the specialist. When I left her cabinet, I was in shock. I'd just discovered that on top of having to stop eating gluten and lactose, I also had to let go of eggs, cauliflower, cabbage, pineapple and apples. How was I going to survive!? She gave me another list of ingredients I was unfamiliar with but that my body would tolerate, such as beetroot, sweet potato, kale and parsnip. She also told me that the energy in my body was mostly yang. My energy was mostly masculine. And you know what? I was proud of it. I was proud to have a masculine energy because I believed at the time that being a girl basically meant you were annoying, boring, hysterical, emotional, stupid, superficial and kind of useless— thank you patriarchal brainwashing. I was super happy about being more yang and decided I would definitely stay like that. I had no idea I was mixing up concepts and doing myself more harm than anything else by thinking like that. But it was a strong rooted belief. My girlfriends and I always used to say, "On n'est pas des filles" meaning "we are not girls." That is, "We are not pussies, hysterical, complicated, superficial, covered with makeup, sensitive girls. Rather we are smart, strong, easy-going badasses." *On n'est pas des filles* was basically our mojo. So, of course, having more yang energy proved I was more in my masculine; I undoubtedly belonged to my group of girlfriends who were "not girls." My friend, who was also more yang, thought I might have been more yin, so I was super proud to tell her I was not. Phew ... I could still belong to the group. I had no clue having excess yang actually meant I was out of balance and a victim of patriarchy. It took me another nine years to understand that and be willing to change it.

In 2020, the year of chaos and forced lockdowns, I got tired of doing, thinking and pushing. I felt a little stuck but kept going as I didn't know how else to manage my coaching business and my life overall. I felt more and more misaligned. And felt the lack of excitement and joy build up. I didn't want to let go of what I had already built and believed was right for me, yet something inside was inviting me to slow down and reflect deeper on what I wanted for my life.

Concurrently, for about eight months, I often dreamt the same dream. I would be walking the streets of a beautiful, luxurious city, like Paris or New York, and meet a man alongside a park. He would bring me into a hotel room, kiss me, undress me and tell me he wanted to marry me. I would say that I couldn't because I was already committed to someone else. I would wake up terrified, feeling like I just made the biggest mistake of my life. It was very confusing. At first, I thought it stemmed from anticipation about remarrying only two years after my divorce, but after our beautiful wedding by the river, the dream continued even more often. I knew I had to understand what this dream was trying to tell me.

I hired a very skilled dream expert, Amala Klep. She helped me see that these two beings in my dream were my inner masculine and inner feminine. My masculine was seductive, very determined, focused, leading and somewhat abusive toward my feminine. My feminine was seduced at first but suddenly felt pressured and fearful. It was too much, too soon, too strong, and she was already committed to something else.

That dream was my wake-up call.

I realized my inner masculine had been ignoring my feminine for a very, very long time. My whole life probably. He thought he knew what she wanted and would deliver it to her without verifying. Sometimes my feminine would scream and make me drop university to sign up for a theatre school, but then the masculine would always come back with needs like safety, security, being seen, being important and being useful. It was time to listen to my inner feminine and try to figure out what she was already committed to. I started to recognize this dream as my soul calling for alignment because my ego had been so strongly leading the way for 33 years.

I let go. I stopped. I worked less, dropped social media, TV and books for 30 days and went on a quest to reconnect with my feminine. I tried to understand who she was, how she functioned, and I invited her to lead the way. I followed her desires and started going more inward instead of being busy all the time. I learned to stay still, be bored and enjoy it. I learned to recognize my inner beauty. I learned to let go of what does not serve me. I learned to go with the flow and be a channel for Life. I learned to surrender so deeply that I would start to see synchronicities and signs everywhere. My only actions would be to respond to them.

During that process of slowing down and going inward, I also got pregnant. What better way to reconnect with your body, your intuition and your feminine energy than through a pregnancy? What better way to understand how much of a channel for Life you are than by creating Life in your womb? I felt blessed. My pregnancy taught me how to be the divine feminine again. While preparing to birth a beautiful human being, I prepared to birth a new way of living, a new self, a new Life.

I learned that the feminine is meant to lead. She's meant to express her desires, and the masculine is there to give her what she wants. She's the visionary, he's the executor. She's the creator, he's the provider. Because the masculine comes from the feminine, she starts, he follows. She's the creator of all. She's the Source. She is. He does. Like the soul who whispers our deepest desires to us, our ego is the channel for their execution.

- How often do you allow her to lead your life?
- How often do you allow yourself to receive instead of give?
- How often do you express your deepest desire and then wait for the aligned action to come through?

You Are a Mango Tree

Healing and awakening your feminine energy are necessary to

start living with more ease, joy and abundance. To embody your soul's purpose. To allow yourself to be the great creatrix that you are. To connect with your divine power within. To live in bliss every second of every day. You might think that I'm dreaming and that this is inaccessible. Hang on before you close this book.

Let's think about Nature for a second and take a closer look at trees. Trees grow naturally without effort, right? Whether it rains, snows, blows or storms, they have solid roots that keep them grounded. They might bend, but they don't break. When winter comes, they lose their leaves without question. They regrow them a few months later. Then they create flowers, fruits and nuts. They produce in abundance. They *are* cyclical abundance.

Do you know how many mangos a mango tree can produce in a year? Up to 500 in its tenth year. Five hundred mangos. How amazing! That's definitely more than enough. You might wonder what the mango tree and feminine energy have in common? Well, everything. Because the mango tree comes from Mother Earth. It is pure feminine energy. The mango tree shows us the main characteristics of feminine energy:

- Follows the path of least resistance, of ease.
- Surrenders.
- Is grounded, calm.
- Is flexible.
- Is creative.
- Has a unique gift or talent.
- Is abundant.
- Moves in cycles and doesn't rush them.
- Brings joy and pleasure.
- Is magnetic.

Can we say that this beautiful mango tree succeeds in its life's purpose and fulfills its mission with success? I assume you're nodding and saying "yes." So why wouldn't your feminine energy likewise lead the way with purpose and success? You aren't very different from the mango tree. You are the mango tree. You are Nature itself. Created by her and creating her over and over again. You are the cycle of Life and have the cycle of Life within you. Isn't it time to surrender to all that wisdom and perfection?

Chapter 3

Healing the Feminine and Masculine Within Ourselves

Before you can embody and vibrate that beautiful, feminine mango tree frequency, you are invited to embark on a healing journey. This healing journey starts now, with this book. Maybe you have already started this journey? In this case, I bow to your wisdom and courage. Let's bring you further along on this hilly path.

When Your Body Talks to You

Healing means scarring your wounds, whether they are emotional, mental or spiritual. But these wounds also translate into physical issues such as depression, burnout, anxiety, chronic illness, eating disorders, broken bones, back pain, etc., which typically show up when you're out of alignment and living from your wounded feminine or masculine. The physical wounds are the tip of the iceberg. They're the call of your soul for change.

Because you are made of pure energy and your physical, emotional, mental and spiritual bodies are intertwined, the physical struggle is the first you'll notice. It's the most concrete, material way your being can express that something is off and needs attention. You'll wake up one day with lower back pain or a sore throat. Yes, you can focus on these symptoms, but the most potent and long-lasting healing comes from addressing their root cause: the emotional, mental or spiritual wound. Your physical pain is very often a clue to an underlying emotional, mental or spiritual blockage.

Ask yourself what happened in the last 48 hours before the physical pain showed up. It's a simple but powerful exercise, so grab your **workbook** (see Contents) and ask yourself the following three questions in Exercise 2 to understand what your body is trying to say to you:

1. What event triggered me in the past two days?
   ○ Did someone say/do something that hurt me?
   ○ Did I hold myself back from saying/doing something?
   ○ Did I receive particular news?
2. How did it make me feel? Did I welcome the emotion or push it back?
3. What was I thinking about myself then? What belief about myself showed up?

Another way to connect with the deeper root of your physical pain is through specialized books, such as *Heal your Body A-Z*, by Louise Hay, or the *Encyclopedia of Ailments and Diseases*, by Jacques Martel. These books identify the psychosomatic pattern related to your medical condition. You'll discover which fear, suppressed emotion, mask, behaviour, limiting belief, identity or spiritual block invites you to deepen your inner work.

Though these blocks might each impact you differently, they have one thing in common: they keep you away from your true divine essence. Healing your divine feminine and divine masculine means letting go of all these layers you added around your soul in order to stay safe. By freeing yourself from pain, beliefs and fears, deconditioning and falling in love with yourself again, you reconnect with your true power, wisdom and purpose. You embody your true authentic self and start living a more soul-led life.

But, as you can guess, it doesn't happen in one day. It's a journey where you are the captain of the boat. You decide whether to keep going or to pause. You might decide to consult a compass every once in a while to set a better course by working with a therapist, coach, healer or refer to a book. And that's great! But remember that the compass can only show you the way—you're the one steering the boat. A guide can't do the work for you. Reading, listening or consulting is not enough. Devoting yourself with self-compassion to your healing with small actions day after day is how you'll make progress. It can be as little as 1 percent of your day. Mini steps every day will bring you far. You'll feel resistance, for sure; you'll want to let go of this work that is pushing you out of your comfort zone; you'll look in another direction sometimes and you'll want to stop when the sun is out of the clouds. And that's ok. Sometimes it's by stopping to enjoy the sunshine on the deck of your boat that you'll notice the island you are hoping to reach. You'll then be able to start again with more clarity, determination and direction. Or maybe you'll decide to stay for several days on your sunny deck. And that's ok too as long as you are fully aware of it. Set sail again when you feel ready. Because your healing depends on you. And you alone. No one else. You're the captain of your boat; no one else knows your boat better than you, which direction it is headed or how to navigate it. Your transcendence depends on how much inner work you're willing to devote yourself to every day. Just keep going despite the resistance, discomfort and frustration. The more you approach this work with compassion for yourself, the easier it will be. But do not worry, you have received several years to explore this journey. A whole lifetime actually. Several lifetimes even.

Wounded Feminine Characteristics

The wounded feminine, also called the unintegrated feminine, dark feminine or shadow feminine, is an energy you carry, whether or not you are aware of it. Every woman carries this energy within herself. No woman is exempt. But some act from it consistently without any awareness, while others see themselves in it every once in a while.

We call it the wounded feminine because when your soul birthed from Source, you felt a sense of disconnection that left a spiritual wound in your energy field. Masculine energy is about individualisation and differentiation, whereas the feminine is all about community and oneness. Since then, this part of yourself has been craving connection. That consistent search for oneness has a dark side: the wounded feminine who negates herself to experience unity. Another experience reinforced that feeling of disconnect: the separation from the womb of your mother; once more, you felt pulled away. Then, as you grew into a child and teenager, any sort of abuse, violence, big T or little T trauma convinced you that you needed to be loved in order to be safe. You started negating yourself, hiding parts of yourself and giving your power away to feel at one with someone else again. And every time you gave your power away to feel that sense of connection, it deepened the wound. With time, you forgot you were still connected to Source through your soul; you forgot your own power and sought that oneness by trying to fit in, asking others for approval, needing others, hiding parts of yourself, allowing others to push you down, not speaking your truth, etc. The millennia of masculine domination finally made sure this wounded energy would become your new normal. And if it's not from your life, you carry this wound from your grandmothers and from the collective. As you sense it now, it is a heavy wound to carry because it is not only yours. It's a wound we all carry as it has been passed down from generation to generation. Big breath in…. Big breath out….

Get to know the main characteristics of this energy and you can consciously choose to change your behaviour, to love yourself more in these areas of your life and to heal fully. This book, its teachings and exercises, will increase your awareness of the energetic imprint of the wounded feminine and diminish the impact it has on your life. This will allow all your power, creativity and gifts to come through. You are about to become the magnetic, talented, intuitive, unique, powerful woman you were always meant to be.

Let's examine how acting from your wounded feminine looks. This list might trigger emotions, so address it with self-compassion and from a place of no judgment. Remember, we all carry some wounded feminine energy, me included!

- You like to control situations and people. You want things to go a certain way and feel unsafe when you're not in control.
- You experience fear and anxiety, which underlie certain choices.
- You struggle with your emotions because you don't realize you can be in a healthy relationship with your anger, sadness and frustration.
- You are arrogant every once in a while, which is actually a false sense of confidence.
- You worry easily and think of worst-case scenarios.
- You tend to ask others for approval, advice, love or protection.
- You can be co-dependent.
- You seduce to get what you want, which makes you manipulative.
- You're inauthentic; you struggle to say how you feel or speak your truth; you say "yes" when you mean "no."
- You tend to play the victim.
- You struggle to set boundaries.
- You seek connection, oneness to feel good.

If you recognize yourself in some of these behaviours, that's alright. Be gentle with yourself. These behaviours have been passed through generations; developed as protections from your ego; or have been learned from parents, teachers, friends, movies, books, etc. They're also mostly unconscious. So, if you admitted, "Yes, I can be like that," you're already a step ahead. Having awareness around these behaviours is the first step to healing and awakening the divine feminine within yourself.

If you'd like to let go of these behaviours and reconnect with your power, download your **workbook** (see Contents) if you haven't done so yet and print it. We'll start shifting from your wounded feminine to your divine feminine with Exercise 3. Before you start, remember it is not about being perfect or ultra-disciplined; small changes made with repetition make a huge difference in the long run.

Realignment Exercise

1. Today, I recognize myself in this characteristic: ....
2. Say out loud: "I can see I have been / I am being ....
   But I am safe in this present moment. I thank myself for being aware of this and choose another behaviour instead."
3. Close your eyes and remember a moment where you were your best version. Feeling safe, limitless, connected to your joy, purpose and power. Visualize that for a minute.
4. What clothes are you wearing in this visualization? ....
5. What emotions are you feeling in this visualization? ....
6. If you knew you were deeply loved, and nothing could go wrong, how would this best version of you choose to behave instead? ....
7. Say out loud three times: "I choose to................ (act with this higher version of myself) today."

The next time you notice one of these behaviours, slow down, take a deep breath, find a private space and do this exercise. If you noticed the behaviour in hindsight, that's ok. Simply do this exercise later. Your brain will get the same benefits as doing it in a present situation. Close your eyes and see yourself acting from your highest self, like you would have acted if you knew you were safe, loved and nothing could go wrong. By visualizing acting from your highest self, you create new neural pathways in your mind that will inevitably change your behaviours and actions in your future reality. It's all about practice and bringing awareness to your own behaviour by choosing how to act or how you could have acted, instead. Be gentle with yourself, you are trying to change years of patterns. Rome wasn't built in one day!

The more you practice this exercise, the more you will move away from your wounded feminine and align with your divine feminine. If you'd like more guidance on healing yourself, I invite you to look at my first book, *The Self-Healing Spiral*. It helps women heal trauma through the power of self-love. There are many books that offer guidance on healing emotional wounds, rewiring limiting beliefs, increasing self-love and uncovering your true essence.

Healed Feminine Energy Characteristics

As you heal more and more, day after day, you will get closer to the empowered divine feminine that lies within. Through the practical exercises and tips in Part 2 of the book, you will develop the following healed feminine energy behaviours, which in turn will reconnect you with your womb, the seat of your sovereignty, creativity and soul. This will inevitably lead you to experience more success, abundance, joy, alignment, purpose and impact.

○ You know how powerful you are, and you use that power to serve.

- You actively listen to those you serve, support and help.
- You have a healthy relationship with your emotions, especially anger.
- You are very compassionate toward yourself and others.
- You flow through life effortlessly; you get what you want with ease.
- You are creative, allowing ideas and projects to flow through you.
- You are very intuitive and hold a lot of wisdom within yourself.
- You surrender fully, trusting yourself and Life.
- You are authentic, always speaking your truth and showing yourself fully.
- You are magnetic; amazing things happen to you daily.
- You are receptive, open to receiving more compliments, love, abundance.
- You are reflective; you reflect on your day, your life in general; you like to daydream.
- You embrace your cycles and natural rhythms.
- You are grounded, calm, connected to Nature.
- You collaborate, gather, live in connection with and support others.

Knows Her Power

What is true power? In French, "power" is translated in two different ways and means two different things: "le pouvoir" and "la puissance." The first definition relates to control or influence you have over others; the second relates to the strength, resourcefulness and wisdom you hold within yourself. You can inspire or share it with others with no intention of controlling or influencing them. This second kind of power is true sovereignty and empowers others to be their own sovereign too. At its foundation is your connection to your divine self and to Source itself. As a divine feminine being, you are powerful, strong, limitless, wise and resourceful, and you serve others with that energy. You know you are a sovereign being.

Actively Listens

The divine feminine is an active listener. When you listen to someone while in your divine feminine energy, you hold space for them. You naturally make the other feel safe and confident to express her/his vulnerability. You put all your attention on the person who's talking. Turning off the thoughts in your mind, you do not think of what you're going to say once the other is finished. You actively listen with your heart. You give all your attention, trusting that when it is time for you to speak, you will find the right words that need to be spoken.

In your daily life that may look like listening to your friends when they need support. But it also means that you listen to your environment, your clients, your community. You listen to them with care and are able to understand their underlying needs. It is by listening actively to your clients and those you serve that you create an abundant business and life. And the divine feminine is all about creating abundance because she is creative and abundant herself.

Healthy Relationship with Her Emotions

Your emotions are created by situations and people, as well as thoughts and imagination. Whatever the trigger, it brings up physical sensations you identify as emotions. The divine feminine knows that emotions are guides. They show you where there's potential for growth or where you must set more boundaries out of love for yourself. In the divine feminine, when your emotions show up, you observe, welcome and thank them. You do not identify with them or try to give them meaning straight away. You feel them fully first. Then you learn from them. You handle them with self-compassion and detachment.

You know that sadness exists to free you from something, and relief is always on the other side of a good cry. So, you allow yourself to cry whenever you feel sadness arise. You let go of the disappointment, hurt, expectation or hope, and allow the tears to roll down your cheeks. You know how healing they are.

You know that anger exists to help you set boundaries. You feel it fully and express it through journaling, exercising, moving or screaming into a pillow. Then you take action and express your boundary to the other person in a calm but firm way. You respect that the other might not see things your way, and you fully accept that. There is no right or wrong as everyone has a different perspective and truth. But you choose to respect yours by expressing what is and is not ok for you.

You know that fear exists to keep you safe. Fear is a natural emotion you will experience throughout your whole life, but you choose not to give it your power. Whenever you feel fear, you instead assess the situation and the risks. Then you tune into your body to seek deeper wisdom from your intuition and learn which direction to go. You also know that fear shows you your next growing edge.

You know frustration/bitterness/disappointment just mean that you are out of alignment. You choose to bring yourself back. You understand that behind these emotions probably lies a deeper fear that things might not go the way you think they should go. So, you embrace your fear of things going wrong and surrender to a higher power that has your best interest at heart. You don't see the whole plan that's at work, but you trust there is one.

Compassionate

When your divine feminine is healed, you act with compassion for yourself and others. You embrace both the feminine and masculine aspects of compassion that teach unconditional self-love. Whenever you face a challenging emotion, you approach it with compassion and ask yourself:

- How will I release the emotion I feel now?
- How will I soothe myself, calm my body?
- How will I validate what I feel?

These three questions cover the feminine, feeling side of compassion. But allowing yourself to feel and care for the emotion is not enough. The emotion is a clue for you to take action too. This is why self-compassion also has a masculine aspect. After attending to your emotion, ask yourself:

- How will I prevent this from happening again/being hurt again?
- What are the other needs I have and how will I fulfill them?
- How will I do all this with kindness toward myself instead of self-criticism?

If a relationship with a boss, colleague or client brings up triggers, you are fully compassionate with yourself. You start with journaling to release the emotion. In the divine feminine, you always begin by welcoming the emotion and fully feeling it. Next you take a warm bath, go for a walk or practice some yin yoga because the mind calms down when the body is calm. You validate everything you feel by recognizing how you feel. "Yes, I am feeling … and it is perfectly normal that I feel this way." Then you act and express a boundary/request/need to the other person. You check in with yourself to see if you have other needs at that moment—taking a day off, spending some quality time with a loved one, cleaning your house, going for a massage. You, of course, embrace this whole process with kindness toward yourself and let go of any self-judgment.

Flows Effortlessly

You might think that flow means ease and continuously receiving. In part it does. But the truth is that flow is not a laid-back energy. Flow means doing effortlessly while embracing your cycles, the ebbs *and* flows of your life. When you reach a high, navigating flow is effortless. Lots of things come your way, you respond to them, you do what feels good, you are inspired and everything you touch transforms into gold, like your fingertips are magic wands!

But flow also slows. It can be still and invite you to be still. The river of Life does not always flow intensely. During the dry spell after a huge rainy season, the sun makes the river shallow and much slower. These periods of rest and reset are when the magic happens. You are being asked to stop, to integrate, to feel, to go inward. And it is uncomfortable because you're so used to "doing." You worry that if you don't do anything, your business/project/life will just stand still. That fear comes from the "work hard, play hard" mantra that we've been fed since childhood. Well, that's false. That fear weakens when you embrace your divine feminine energy. Instead, the healed feminine has you flow and surrender to every season and every rhythm of your river. Embrace your winter. Know that this season is mandatory for spring to happen. You don't see the flowers getting ready in the vines, but they are. So be patient, stop doing and going against the slow flow of your river.

Creative

Your feminine energy is naturally creative. You create life in your womb, and not just perfect little babies. So many other projects actually come from your womb, whether or not you realize it. As a feminine being, you incubate, transform and create something new from whatever comes your way. As author Erick Gray says:

> Whatever you give a woman, she will make it greater.
> If you give her sperm, she gives you a baby.
> You give her a house, she gives you a home.
> You give her groceries, she gives you a meal.
> You give her a smile, she'll give you her heart.
> She multiplies and enlarges what is given to her.

Feminine energy constantly creates when she is connected to Source. She is inspired. Pause here for a second and think about what "inspiration" really means. Inspiration, or "in-spirit," means taking in the spirit that is around you and allowing it to birth through you. When you are inspired, you take in the energy of Source, transform it within yourself and create something unique from it. You are naturally and effortlessly connected to Source. You channel it and allow it to be expressed through you. Whatever the idea, it comes to you and only you for a specific reason. You are a vessel of Life.

Inspiration also means "inhaling," which I love because it shows how language actually proves that Spirit is all around. We breathe it in second by second and stay alive thanks to it. Thanks to allowing Spirit to flow through us. Thanks to being a channel of Life.

While creativity has a very upward energy because it receives ideas from Source through the three upper chakras, it also has a very downward energy from rooting those ideas into matter. Inspired creativity is more than just having ideas come out of the blue. It is also about bringing those ideas into reality. Because feminine energy is Earth energy, ideas are both inspired and grounded. Creativity does not remain in the high spheres of thought; feminine energy births new ideas into Life.

Though the masculine is considered the do-er, the healed feminine also takes action. She moves from a place of inspired creation, a place of surrendering to her desires and impulses coming from her womb. She transforms, grounds and gives life with flow, ease and in divine timing, which means slowly and when she feels that the time is right. The masculine brings her the environment, the structure and the foundation to create safely. He makes sure that she has everything she needs for her creative process to unfold. She has the vision; he completes the "to-do list" and provides the tools. Finally, she follows her desires as to when and how to take action on these tasks. It's an ongoing dance. She can't create without him, and he doesn't know what to do without her.

That's why it is so important to create sacred union between your masculine and your feminine to allow all your ideas and projects to flourish successfully and abundantly.

Intuitive

Intuition. We all have it. And it comes from the feminine energy we hold within. To connect to your natural intuition, you need to connect to your body and be in a state of receiving. That intuition gives you direct access to the wisdom of your soul. You hear, see or feel your body's cues leading you to the right next step. Once you learn how powerful intuition is, you stop using logic to make decisions. You are confident that your intuition is all-knowing whereas your mind only has limited perspective. Intuition-based decisions might be seen as irrational or illogical, but you trust the guidance of your body.

I remember feeling a deep, illogical desire to move to Vancouver when I was living in Quebec for a few months. Specifically, I was in Montreal to study energy healing at the Institute of the healer and author, Dolores Lamarre. After that year, I was supposed to return home to Belgium to open an energy healing practice there. It would have been the most logical choice. My network was in Belgium, and I was already building a clientele every time I went back. But it felt restrictive, cold, dark. Every time I thought about returning, my body shut down. Vancouver, on the other hand, felt warm, expansive, open. My boyfriend was potentially going to move there, but I wasn't sure if we would move in together, how easily I could get a work visa and create a community of clients or if I'd even like this city I had never been to before. It was a scary, illogical choice. But my gut kept pushing me in that direction. So, I went.... I moved to British Columbia with no idea of what awaited me. And now I can see why. In a few months, we got married, got blessed with a beautiful son, and I got my permanent residency, made amazing friends and built a thriving business. It was the best choice for my soul's purpose and fulfillment, but I could not know or see that through the narrow perspective of my logical mind. I could only feel the expansion and warmth my soul was sending to my body.

Your intuition is all-knowing; it always shows you the right next step. You will learn how to awaken the gift of intuition further in this book.

Surrenders

If you are old-school, open a dictionary to the word "surrendering," and you will read "ceasing to resist" below the word. Surrendering brings up the image of the white flag in a battle. Stopping the fight. Letting go. But there is a slight misunderstanding about what it actually means in a spiritual context. It has nothing to do with abandoning the fight. It's about letting go of your resistance, your tight grip on something you desire, while maintaining a loose grip and letting things go their own way. Nature knows the best and easiest course to bring you where you want to be, so the divine feminine chooses to surrender to it. You have a loose grip, embrace what is, trust what is and act only when you feel called to. You don't fight; you don't resist the natural flow of life or force anything. Rather, you embrace, trust and act when your heart tells you to.

On a scale from 1 to 10, how good are you at surrendering? Not trying to control people, situations or outcomes? Trusting that whatever happens is for your highest good even if you can't see it right now? Not so easy, right? You might struggle to surrender because of your need to control. Control is a protective mechanism that many of us adopted in our early childhood. Control comes from the ego that wants you to be safe. So, whenever you feel unsafe, you exert control to bring yourself back to a safe space. It goes even further. You actually control people, situations and outcomes because, deep down, you don't trust yourself. You don't know if you have the skills, knowledge or strength to face a possible bad outcome. You fail to see how resourceful you are and that whatever happens in your life, you will figure it out, heal and transcend it. You don't trust yourself and might even feel inadequate, as if you don't know enough, do enough, or are enough.

This sense of inadequacy is one of the deepest human fears and wounds. It disconnects you from your wisdom. It disconnects you from knowing that your greatest strength actually lies in *not knowing* and surrendering to the idea that the right answer will show up at the right moment in your life. With time and contemplation, this fear of inadequacy transforms into resourcefulness and then into wisdom. You end up living with the paradox that wisdom arrives through not knowing rather than through knowing. And that wisdom gives you access to complete surrender. You are invited to grow your surrender muscle in the next part of this book.

Authentic

The healed feminine is authentic. She says all of what she thinks, shows all of who she is and expresses all of herself in everything she does. It might seem an obvious way of living, but you have years of conditioning that have pushed your uniqueness down. Yet authenticity is key to living your life to the fullest. It is by being fully authentic, fully yourself, that your purpose will come to you and that you will magnetize wealth, success, opportunities and soul sisters. You didn't choose to have a human experience to be someone else. You came here to enjoy yourself fully and simply be yourself.

Part 2 will show you how to awaken the pivotal gift of authenticity in order to start truly living your life instead of surviving in a world you've built with "shoulds," pressures and rules that do not suit you. This gift is the first bridge allowing you to move away from your wounded to your divine feminine.

Magnetic

As you are made of pure energy, you emit and receive energy constantly. Like a magnet, your unique energy attracts or repels certain energies. It attracts matching energies and repels opposite energies. When you embody the energy of joy, you attract events that bring more joy into your life, whether signing a big contract or creating new amazing friendships. Likewise, you repel people who vibrate at the opposite end of the spectrum. People living in fear might trigger you, criticize you, judge you or even reject you. You will also outgrow relationships, jobs, houses and projects when you are no longer an energetical match. This happens naturally, without any conscious effort because you constantly emit energy and the world around you responds to it.

You can consciously amplify your natural magnetism. By working on your own energy, you enhance your power of attraction. Because energy is one, everywhere and connected to all things, the only difference between various frequencies is the speed at which the energy moves. The faster it moves, the higher the frequency. The higher the frequency, the more powerful your magnetism. Paradoxically, you increase the speed of your vibration by slowing down. By doing less and being more, you become less dense, vibrate faster and align with the natural magnetism of the Earth, another feminine element, which amplifies your own magnetism. To tap into the magnetism of Mother Earth, embody all of your divine feminine: flowing, surrendering, receiving, creating, being still. Then you will activate the full potential of your magnetism.

This gift will be further explained in Part 2 where you will discover powerful exercises to amplify your own unique magnetism.

Receptive

Receptivity is, of course, expressing your ability to receive—whether it is help, compliments, love or money. Think of these as different energies responding to how open or closed your receiving channel is. Your receptivity to one thing indicates your receptiveness to everything. So, if you wonder how open your receiving channel is, just observe how easy (or not) it is for you to receive compliments. How do you respond when you receive an unexpected compliment? Do you say "thank you" straight away, or do you freeze and say something else? The more open you are to fully receive compliments, the greater your receptivity for anything else.

Receiving is bonded to masculine energy as he needs to be the one giving so that you, or the feminine aspect of you, can receive.

The basic principle is that your feminine expresses her desires, shares her vision and waits to receive. Then the masculine executes, provides and brings her the object of her desire. That ongoing dance allows the flow of Life to circulate freely; both energies need to stick to their role for it to work. Receiving looks different depending on whether you receive something from yourself or from someone else.

For example: you want more money. As a co-creator, creating your life with the help of an invisible force, you lead with your feminine and allow your co-creator, the Universe, to do the rest. The Universe is the masculine here. Start by asking for what you want; the Universe needs to know, otherwise it can't bring it to you! Be as specific as possible but open to even more or better than what you have in mind. Speak it out loud, write it down, put it on a post-it … and then allow the magic to happen. He will create a whole plan to manifest your desire and will guide you via your intuition should you need to do anything else to receive it. You must stay in your feminine, connected to your intuition and surrendered to divine timing as well, to see the object of your desire turn into reality. But if you attempt to control the "how"— pushing, doing, planning, structuring—you will take over the masculine role and prevent the Universe from giving you what you desire. It is not your job to figure out the how and execute the task. Your only job is to express what you desire and follow the cues of your intuition one after the other. That's how you stay in your feminine and allow the Universe to take the masculine role.

If you hope to receive something from someone else, your husband or partner, for example, it plays out a little differently because the feminine and masculine roles are spread between two people. Let's say your husband loves to cook and look after the house and you're the money-maker. While these roles might make you feel like he's the feminine and you're the masculine of the house, your energies say otherwise. By cooking for you and picking up the groceries from the list you made, he's providing you safety and protection, allowing you to receive a warm meal after you've given all your creativity to a job you love. This is a perfect example of how men can stay in their masculine energy even though they seem to be doing tasks that we wrongly qualify as feminine. So, if you want something else from him, let him know. Like the Universe, he can't read your mind! Ask for what you want, sit back and allow him to bring it to you in his own time without controlling the how. Don't tell him how to cook! Otherwise, you assume the masculine energy and put him in his feminine energy by not allowing him to provide for you. Let him do, in his own way and time, what you have asked, and trust that it will show up when it is ready.

The gift of receiving will be fully developed in the second part of this book.

Reflective

The divine feminine has a reflective nature. She daydreams, she visualizes, she hopes, she creates from her desires, she reflects on the good, the bad, the beautiful, the ugly. She integrates. She transforms. She alchemises ideas into projects, foods into meals. And it all starts with ideas, reflections, thoughts.

Invite reflective moments into your days or weeks to connect with a deeper wisdom you have within. Creating that quiet space in your life to integrate everything that happens—thinking about your past, projecting your future and counting the blessings of the present moment—is very grounding. Reflection gives you clarity about your desires, your needs, your hopes, your next steps. It's that necessary moment of stillness before you can take the aligned action. The right next step.

Cyclical

You are a cyclical being. You live in cycles: beginnings, zeniths, endings. Every day the sun rises, every evening the sun sets. Every month the moon fills and unfills herself. Every year leaves grow on trees and flowers bloom, spreading their amazing smell, colours and pollen, and then fade. The petals fall down and allow the tree, the plant, the flower itself to start a new cycle with a period of rest that looks like nothing is happening from the outside, but with everything happening on the inside.

You too live in permanent change, in permanent movement, flowing from one state to the other. Even if your life looks like it has a routine, deep down, it doesn't. The more you are aware of these changes and phases, and the more you honour them by moving in accordance with your inner rhythms, seasons, cycles and periods, the easier it gets. Move with your energy and follow its guidance instead of fighting against it and struggling through it because someone else told you that's how it was supposed to be done.

Whether you're working for someone else, launching a business or have been running a successful business for several years, connecting and honouring your own rhythms will propel you to achieve much more. Your body holds this wisdom. It has a bright intelligence and knows much better than your mind what is right for you.

Align with the daily cycles of the sun. Align with the monthly cycles of the moon that are directly related to your monthly bleeding. Align with the yearly cycles of the seasons and find your own inner rhythms as well by asking yourself regularly, "What does my body need now? What do I feel like doing right now? What do I want in this present moment?"

I believe it is time to let go of this crazy fast-paced society that makes us believe we have so much to do and so little time. Let's drop the unceasing search of success and instant gratification, stimulated by the fear of not having enough, not being enough. We are enough. And we can achieve much more when we move in accordance with our own energy and rhythm.

Nature shows us how every day. She is abundant, peaceful, successful. She has rhythms and cycles that allow the necessary changes for every stage to unfold. She embraces those changes instead of resisting them. And embraces the periods of rest that are so precious for spring to bloom.

We are Nature as well. When did we disconnect from the trees, the flowers, the moon, thinking we were better? Nature regenerates season after season just like your body does. Nature is perfect just like your body is. Nature is abundant just like your life will be if you allow it to flow and embrace all its cycles.

Grounded

As obvious as it sounds, I want to emphasize that being grounded means being connected to the ground. But more than just being physically connected to Mother Earth, grounding means having your soul connected to Her. She nourishes your whole chakra system and goes from your eighth chakra, just above your crown, to your first, or root, chakra, which in turn connects you to the ground. You are in your whole body, fully present, fully incarnated.

When you are grounded, you are calm. Your emotions don't take over. You're in your body rather than in your mind. You know what's right for you, and this knowing comes from *feeling* what's right for you instead of thinking, and overthinking, it. You hold strong boundaries. You are in your power. You bring your dreams into reality, your ideas into matter. You are joyful and manifest much physical energy because you connect with the stable feminine dynamic energy of the Earth. Fully incarnated, you bring your essence forth. You are also deeply connected to your womb, its sexual, creative power and your unique purpose. In other words, you are embodied. Your soul is in your body and leads your life.

A whole chapter is dedicated to grounding in Part 2 of this book. It will help you awaken this natural state of being that connects you to Earth, improves your health and increases your creativity, intuition and sovereignty.

Collaborative and Supportive

The healed feminine is the opposite of jealous. She loves to gather with other women and celebrates their success with them. She knows that another woman's success only means that hers is getting closer. Seeing success—love, money, health—manifest in someone else's life tells her that her own success is coming into matter soon. She knows that what is meant for her is not going to someone else. So, she supports her women, she collaborates with them, she refers them, she celebrates them.

When you embody healed feminine energy, you love to gather with other women. You create sisterhoods, you share with others how you feel and what you're going through, you gain clarity by talking with your sisters. You also experience more success and fulfillment by being and working with others. "Connection and Community" is the royal road to wealth for the feminine-essence being that you are.

Masculine Energy Characteristics

Your masculine energy also holds wounded and healed characteristics. The wounded masculine is very much focused on safety, competition and ego-driven success. Through the healing of your feminine, you inevitably start healing your masculine as well, as they are connected and intertwined. But the divine feminine needs to be healed and awakened first as the masculine comes from the feminine. The yang is created from the yin. A full discussion of the wounded and healed masculine is outside the scope of this book which focuses on healing and awakening your divine feminine energy. But a brief overview is worthwhile as you need to create sacred union between these two energies.

Embrace yourself with kindness if you express any of the wounded masculine traits. It is probably a nurtured or protective behaviour because you were led to believe you had to behave this way to be safe or loved. Working through the exercises of this book will inevitably start their healing process and lead to sacred union within yourself. You can use the realignment exercise (Exercise 3) from your **workbook** to consciously choose to act from your healed masculine. This practice works equally well for the awakening of the healed feminine as well as the healed masculine.

Ex 3

Behaviours of the Wounded Masculine

- Needs to control the feminine to feel safe because he's afraid of her instability.
- Overreaches.
- Tends to gaslight and be aggressive.
- Avoids, withdraws.
- Competes.
- Abuses.
- Unstable.

- Arrogant.
- Bossy.

Behaviours of the Healed Masculine

- Knows he's an anchor for the feminine.
- Helps her come back into alignment.
- Observant, very present.
- In touch with his feelings.
- Tender.
- Confident.
- Logical.
- Focused.
- Disciplined.
- Honest.
- Accountable.
- Humble.
- Stable and secure.

Chapter 4

Sacred Union and Prosperity

Sacred Union

Our divine feminine and divine masculine need and balance each other. We need both energies within ourselves to accomplish our projects. A woman who is too much in her feminine tends to daydream and never accomplish anything. A woman who is too much in her masculine accomplishes a lot but probably not the right things and exhausts herself along the way.

Quite often, we lead our lives more from one energy than the other, creating a distrust between both parts of ourselves, like conflicting beliefs or fears. This imbalance needs to be reconciled for sacred union to happen.

Sacred union happens in our womb, in our core. This is where we physically create life, when the sperm meets the egg, but it is also an energetical portal to the Source of all creation. When we feel a new idea is right, we feel it in our gut. We feel it in our womb. Our feminine and masculine have met and are ready to create together.

Ex 4

I invite you for a beautiful, very intuitive exercise to recreate that sacred union within yourself. Find Exercise 4 in your **workbook** (see Contents), which you probably have downloaded from my website, to access an audio meditation of this exercise.

Place your hands on your womb to connect with the feminine part of yourself and give her the opportunity to express herself. Here is how you will proceed:

1. Close your eyes and sit in silence, connecting energetically with your womb.
2. Slowly, picture yourself descending 10 steps; with every breath, count each of the 10 steps. Sink into yourself with every step.
3. At the end of the stairs, there's a golden door. Open it.
4. Enter a beautiful garden, walk around for some time and, when you are ready, let your feminine appear to you. Observe how she's dressed, how she holds herself, the look in her eyes.
5. Ask her the following questions and give her time to bring the answers to you:
   - How do you feel?
   - What do you long for?
   - What would you like to say to your partner, the masculine?
   - What do you want to create together?
6. Let your feminine finish what she has to say and when she is done, thank her.
7. Now, allow your masculine to join you. Observe how he is dressed, how he holds himself, the look in his eyes.
8. Ask him:
   - How do you feel?
   - How do you want to support your partner, the feminine?
   - How do you want to protect her so that she can create?
   - What else would you like to say?

You can do this exercise through meditation, by journaling or simply by writing a letter from one energy to the other. To support you in this exercise, and if it resonates with you, I share below the letters my feminine and masculine wrote to each other. If you'd also like to write the letters, write first to your inner masculine from your feminine. As the feminine needs to be healed first so that she can birth a healed masculine, she must lead before he executes.

Create a sacred space for yourself to write these two letters by lighting a candle, listening to relaxing music, grounding yourself and working in a space where you won't be disturbed.

Letter from My Feminine to My Masculine

My dear Masculine,

Thank you for taking the time to read me. I have to admit I have felt very let down these past years. I know you've always wanted to give me the best, but you were so busy all the time, running around from one place to another, trying to prove yourself, trying to protect me, you didn't take the time to ask me what I wanted. I felt like you did not care what I longed for and just decided for both of us what was right.

First, I am grateful you finally heard my cry for help, because I have so much to give to you and so many things I want to do with you. But I can't do them alone; I need you to be more present with me and to listen to me. Can you check in with me more often and make sure your initiatives come from my place of longing rather than your place of neediness?

Next, I need you to recognize my vulnerability. I want you to honour it instead of trying to hide it. It is a proof of great strength to recognize your limits, express your vulnerability and respect your own needs. I know you have tried to protect me from others who judged my vulnerability by trying to push it down, but it is time to express my true self and stop pretending to be someone else. I know we can do this together and I know it will show others they can be themselves and express their vulnerability as well. Thank you for all these years of protection, but now is the time to let go.

Finally, I would like to ask you to invite more fun into our lives. You're so serious all the time. Let's do things we enjoy, relax, laugh, be ridiculous. Life is supposed to be spontaneous, fun. I have great intuition and can show you the path of joy instead of the path of pressure made of things you think we should do. Success and Abundance are at the end of this road as well. I know for sure. So, will you let me guide you more?

From my side, I am committing to trust you from now on. I know that in the past months, I did not give you a lot of room to act because I only wanted you to listen to me. But from now on, I will express more of my desires to give you the direction you seek and then I will trust you. I know you can make things happen; you have already proven to be very determined.

Here are my promises, my vows, to you:
I promise to trust you.
I promise to forgive you if you are impatient or worried.
I promise to take up more space.
I promise to be grateful for everything you provide for me.

Now, let me hug you and show you how much I love you and want to be connected to you. Let's be partners in crime and meet each other where we are at with the innocence of our pure hearts. This would make me the happiest. I know we are going to achieve great things together.

Letter from My Masculine to My Feminine

My dear Feminine, My dear Queen,

Thank you for opening your heart to me. I am only here to serve you and have overstepped when I thought I knew what you wanted. I am happy to see you are ready to trust me again and want to move forward, hand in hand, with me.

My purpose is to serve you, to protect you and it is always easier for me when you can express to me what your deepest desires are. There is nothing that brings me more joy than seeing you in your power, in your light, in your queen-essence. This is when I feel fulfilled and can become your King.

On the days where you feel more emotional and doubt that queen-essence, I am happy to listen to you, to hold space for you, to support you, to ground you and to remind you all is well.

Even though safety and protection are always on my mind, I will remember your request to have more fun and bring more joy into our lives. Always in a safe environment, of course.

My dear Goddess, here are my promises, my vows to you:
I promise to support you and remind you how powerful you are.
I promise to serve you and bring you the object of your desires.
I promise to listen, carefully and compassionately, when you need me to.
I promise to protect you and set boundaries with people, situations or energies that are not in your highest interest.

Love always,
Your King, Your Masculine self

Prosperity from Sacred Union

Now that you are on the way to create sacred union within yourself, abundance and prosperity are just around the corner. Your natural state is to be abundant, to have more than enough in your life. More than enough love, support, energy, friends, opportunities, money.... Prosperity goes a level further. It is a flourishing that also covers all aspects of life, yet it brings even more than abundance. You are here to experience a prosperous life, not to struggle to make ends meet. But your own energy, made of fears, beliefs, worries, unhealed traumas, etc., blocks the flow of natural abundance. As everything in life, your external reality is a reflection of your internal reality. By healing your masculine and feminine energy, and bringing them into sacred union, you will access the flow of prosperity that wants to come your way. This perfect balance realigns you with the natural prosperous state of Life.

Your masculine and feminine energy have several characteristics that I covered in the last pages. The more you act, move, decide and live from their healed vibration, the more you align with abundance. But these energies also each have a gift that is unique to you. And the blend of these two unique gifts has yet another unique energy and signature which is your royal road to prosperity.

Your feminine gift shows you how to connect with your deepest desires, creativity and intuition and be in a receptive state to receive the abundance the masculine provides. You receive what is meant for you when you operate at the level of the feminine's gift. Understand that this gift has to be fully present in your life before you can unlock the masculine gift. The masculine comes from the feminine and exists to serve the feminine, so it is only when you have embodied this feminine gift that your masculine energy can reach its gift frequency and bring you all the prosperity you deserve.

Your masculine gift shows you the structure and foundation of your prosperity. If you don't operate at the level of this gift, you won't live in prosperity because the masculine energy won't be able to provide that abundance to you. Only when this gift is truly embodied will you feel how much Life provides for you.

When acting from the level of both gifts, you make purposeful choices and aligned decisions. You are in sacred union, leading you naturally to prosperity.

To find these unique gifts and create your custom prosperity formula, refer to Exercise 5 in your **workbook** (see Contents). This exercise is meant to guide you in the creation of your unique prosperity energy formula. I hope you have had a chance to print it by now because this exercise is broken into several steps and journaling questions.

I invite and encourage you to lay down this book and take the time to do Exercise 5, as it holds a lot of power to help you unlock prosperity in all areas and at all levels of your life.

Part 2

The Six Gifts of Your Sovereignty

Chapter 5

Why These Six Gifts Lead to Your Sovereignty

Why "Gifts"

Gifts are something you are naturally good at. The divine feminine gifted you six abilities to make the most out of life. They are your tools—pen, journal, laptop, notepad—for the School of Life. These six gifts were, at some point, very innate. But through the conditioning of society, education, trauma and the building of your ego, you probably lost touch with them. The good news is that they're still in you, quietly waiting to reconnect and become part of your everyday life again. It's an awakening to who you are and have always been. But waking up can be painful because it means you recognize you were asleep. And nobody wants to admit they lived asleep, often for several years, maybe most of their life. So, the key to unlock and awaken these natural gifts is to address this second part of the book with self-compassion. Like a child learning to walk again after spending years in bed, you'll fall. You'll struggle. But with your childlike passion and worry-free mind, you'll get up and eventually get there. You will awaken and reconnect with your six gifts. Like everything in life, it's all about practice and belief in yourself.

Gifts are also frequencies, energies, embodiments. By unlocking these six gifts, one after the other, you will reclaim the sovereignty of your own life. You always have been sovereign and now are simply reconnecting with this truth page after page, experience after experience, day after day. These six gifts will become a new way of life for you. A new way of vibrating and expressing your energy through the world. And because everything is energy, the world will respond differently to you, reinforcing your trust in these new frequencies that you emit, this new way of life you embrace. You will remember that you are a sovereign being. An infinite being that lives according to her own truth, in harmony with who she is, shining a light on Earth simply by being and reaching for the stars with ease, pleasure and joy.

And when you fully embody the frequencies, you will receive gifts from Source. You will align with the natural abundance of the Universe, allowing yourself to receive what was simply waiting for you to be ready.

How They Lead to Sovereignty

Sovereignty is the embodiment of your highest self. It's being in your true power, in your unique energy, allowing Source to come through you for your highest good and the good of all those around you. Sovereignty is also remembering that you are a unique expression of Source itself and that your power lies in that connection with Source. Like the poet Rumi beautifully puts it, "You are not a drop in the ocean but the whole ocean in a drop."

Sovereignty comes from the feminine, as the feminine is the first energy, the leading energy, the birthing energy, the yin that creates the yang. So, it is through reconnecting with that feminine energy that you reconnect with your sovereignty. Your true power lies in your womb, your physical and energetical womb. The womb is not just a place that births babies. It's an energetical portal giving you access to Source. It's the portal through which Source flows, transforming you into a vessel. That portal, coming from your womb, the crib of your feminine intuition, connects you with Source and this connection is your sovereignty.

The six gifts leading to your sovereignty are rooted in this feminine energy. As you awaken them, one after the other, they will heal your divine feminine and help you embody this sacred energy. Page after page, you will reconnect with your wisdom, your womb, your sovereignty, which will allow you to live in alignment and move from force to flow, hustle to ease, lack to abundance and emptiness to purpose.

The Gifts Revealed

The six gifts are very intertwined and build upon each other. The order in which I take you through them is not a coincidence. You need authenticity to unlock magnetism. You need a certain magnetism to connect deeper with your intuition, and so on. To be able to teach the gifts, I had to understand them at a core level. But Life guided me through the necessary experiences to feel them and write about them. It was a whole process of surrender—one of the gifts I was most uncomfortable with at first. How could I be writing something interesting and new about surrender? There's already a lot of powerful literature out there about this gift. But I knew it was not about me. I had to let go of my ego, my fears, my own self-judgment to receive the teachings, one after the other. And that's what happened. Like a class you attend week after week, I received download after download. My own life taught me very deep lessons about authenticity, magnetism, and then surrender. Yet writing the second part of this book felt a little bit like a game of charades. I would follow and experience clues. Then I would receive a download; the dots would connect, and I would understand the teaching at a deeper level. I would come upon a video that would attract my attention, watch it and find the answer to a question. I would have a conversation with a coaching client and suddenly have a breakthrough while hearing myself speak. I would feel called to record a new solo episode for my podcast without any notes and feel the depths of the gifts of intuition and surrender. I would experience relationship issues and learn something new about the gift of receiving.

The first message I received in the clear dream I quoted in the Introduction was about authenticity. I needed to be authentic if I wanted to write this book. At first, I felt uncomfortable writing about the gift of authenticity. Yes, I was already on the journey of becoming fully myself, but I still was holding back a little. Yet in that message, I was challenged to go deeper, to speak up, even if it seemed scary, even if it would push people away, even if it would scare some people off. How can you write or teach about a topic if you don't fully embody it? You can't. And you shouldn't. This first gift taught me it was time to step up, to show more of myself, to be more authentic, to talk from my heart even if it attracted critics, rejections, judgments. It most definitely meant I would finally be authentic to myself and my true voice. This first gift was necessary for me to heal more of the wounded feminine energy I still carried in order to write this book and channel the rest of the teachings. Of course, it's not so surprising. It's just divinely planned. Perfect, as always. And I definitely see that perfection in hindsight. It makes me smile at how smart the divine plan always is. We honestly have no clue sometimes.

As you go through the book, you will experience this as well. Life will present learning opportunities because it's how Life works. This book is a living transmission to be experienced through your whole sensory body. It has to be understood at a physical, energetical and heart level, rather than through the eyes and the understanding of the mind. Therefore, I invite you to read Part 2 in the order it is presented. Take time to integrate every teaching and do the exercises from the book and **workbook** (see Contents). Allow yourself to revisit certain paragraphs if they don't initially hit home. Embrace the experiences and challenges that suddenly pop up and are probably (definitely!) related to whichever gift you are studying. The journey you embark on right now, with these pages, is not a journey of the mind. It's a journey of the body, the heart, the womb. It's a feminine process about feminine healing. Reading this book itself is a healing experience of openness, surrender, receptivity, intuition, body connection, cycles, ups and downs. Embrace it all; it is a beautiful journey, a gift to yourself. And it will be perfectly imperfect.

Finally, I'd love to underline that this book is about you and for you, the women, men and the world of tomorrow. I'm merely the channel bringing these unique teachings to you. And I am deeply honoured and humbled Source chose me. But now these teachings choose you. They drew you to this book for a reason. Make these teachings yours, play with them, experience them and allow them to change you at your core. They will deeply impact your life if you let them. They will guide you on the path of becoming the abundant, joyful, successful sovereign you were always meant to be. They will move you from force to flow, from hustle to ease, from power to sovereignty.

"You need to bring all of yourself to life."

–Glennon Doyle

Chapter 6

The Gift of Authenticity

Closing the Doors of Survival

Being authentic is a demanding path. From our first breath, we fight for survival. This survival depends on being loved and ... fitting in. A baby does not survive if it is not loved. A baby does not survive if it is left alone. Being part of the wolf pack—to fit in—assures survival; being out of it assures death. It's innate. As we grow into teenagers and adults, the time of survival fades away. We don't need others to survive anymore. We become independent enough to live. But the need to fit in and to be loved is so ingrained in us that it has become our natural operating mode. And we are mostly unaware of it. Therefore, we behave like others and dim or hide parts of ourselves. Men and women are laughed at, rejected, criticized, tortured or worse, killed, for their differences which reinforces our survival mask we unconsciously think we need. We become independent adults with a dependent child set of beliefs. We do our best to fit in, even though we are truly past the age where our life depends on others.

As a result of these survival needs that we have unnecessarily brought into our adult lives, women negate themselves and follow the rules in place instead. Anything more than average has been suppressed. About 20 years ago, I was visiting my grandparents in the Belgian countryside for some afternoon tea and cake. My sweet grandmother, Marie-Rose, was dressed in a grey suit and said to me, "I know I'm not wearing a skirt today. Your grandfather isn't happy about it, but I am so much more comfortable in these pants. Don't say anything about it, please." I was in shock. In a few words, she perfectly embodied the famous French quote, "Sois belle et tais-toi." Which means "Be beautiful and shut up." I could not believe my ears. Taking the time to say this to me meant she felt like she was crossing a boundary. And she felt so uncomfortable about daring to give herself a little comfort that she had to express that discomfort to someone, as if she was looking for permission. If she wasn't permitting herself to wear pants whenever it pleased her, what else wasn't she allowing herself? What else was she suppressing? What else was she hiding? All of herself probably.… I still remember that day as if it was yesterday.

Even though most women today know that they are more than just beautiful bodies, a lot of our behaviours are still rooted in this patriarchal pressure, this need to fit in, to follow the rules and to do what's expected of us. Being authentic is challenging. It thwarts the survival needs our great-great-grandmothers have passed down to us from generation to generation. Authenticity sounds almost like a rebellious act. And it is. A rebellion against patriarchy. A rebellion against fear. A rebellion against our own beliefs that led us to limit our lives to survival. Authenticity allows us to breathe, to be, to live.

Authenticity is the secret key that closes the doors of survival and opens the doors of Life.

Opening the Doors of Life

Authenticity means being true to yourself. It means showing who you are without playing roles or hiding parts of yourself. Saying what you think without any fear. Sharing your gifts without restraint. Expressing how you feel with innocence and vulnerability. Being authentic is pure. Free of any conditioning, mask, fear or agenda. And that demands a lot of healing, courage and resilience.

One of my spiritual teachers, Makhosi Hefisah Nejeser, says, "The part of yourself that you believe is too much—too noisy, too weird, too creative, too different—that part that you are suppressing, is actually the reason why you're here." It's the part you are meant to show the world. And the more you embody it, the more you will vibrate your innate essence and unlock your purpose, attract soul clients, partners, friends, business opportunities and have an amazing life. This part of you is the key to everything you desire. This authenticity is key to living a purposeful life. It opens the doors of Life; it is as simple as this.

Sometimes, we need to be close to death to allow ourselves to live in full authenticity. We remember how precious life is and how pointless it is to fight ourselves in order to please everyone, fit in and be loved. Anita Moorjani shares her near-death experience in her book, *Dying to Be Me*. Her words beautifully illuminate how the purpose of life and the only way to find our unique purpose is simply to be ourselves: "I felt as though I had a purpose to fulfill. I perceived that I wouldn't have to go out and search for what I was supposed to do, it would unfold for me. . . . I simply had to allow it to unfold. To access the state of allowing the only thing I had to do is to be myself. I realized all I ever had to do is be myself. . . . I knew that realizing this meant never being afraid of who we are. . . . The only purpose of life is to be ourself, live our truth, and be the love that we are."

Give yourself the gift of Life and welcome authenticity now. In your downloaded **workbook** (see Contents), contemplate the three questions of Exercise 6. Set aside this book and give yourself ample time to do this exercise in the **workbook** or in your journal.

Ex 6

Authenticity Contemplation

- What part of you is "too much"?
- What aspects of your life do you hide, even just a little, instead of showing all of yourself?
- How do you embody the pressure of "be beautiful and shut up"? In what ways do you behave as a "good girl" rather than a "bad girl"?

The Three Feminine Wounds

A lack of authenticity comes from the wounded feminine who has forgotten how powerful she is. In fact, she gives her power away through small everyday behaviours like overeating, overworking, overgiving, overcaring, overworrying and overpleasing. In our wounded feminine energy, we struggle with self-love, so we seek it outside. We struggle with self-confidence, so we ask for advice. We struggle with surrender, so we control everything we say, eat or do. We struggle with our own uniqueness and creativity, so we copy others. Our lack of authenticity makes us look more like everyone else, and less like ourselves. We wear masks. We pretend. We shy away from our unique essence. We might suppress it so much that we don't even know who we really are. So, we take quizzes, read books and attend spiritual retreats in hopes of reconnecting with that hidden authentic self. We yearn for someone to tell us who we are, why we're here and answer the hard question: "Who am I?" The pressure underlying that question is intense. And it manifests through constant self-doubt. Am I good enough? Is this good enough? I hope they like me. Do I look good in this video?

Should I say this? Maybe I should just shut up? Maybe I should wear something else? Isn't this a little too much? What are they going to think? Is this the right thing to do?

Lack of authenticity is an uncomfortable, even painful, burden. But it's one you might choose to hold on to because it's familiar. You're used to it, and you can cope with it. It might even feel less dangerous than living authentically and risking public humiliation. But isn't that an expensive price to pay to survive?

One day you tire of paying so much to push yourself away. It doesn't make any sense anymore. You realize you should actually be paid for being yourself because your true gifts lie in your authenticity. It's how to best serve others too. Your authenticity allows others to be themselves. When you're vulnerable, you allow others to be vulnerable. When you're creative, you allow others to create. When you speak your truth, you amplify everyone's truth. When you're fully and authentically yourself, you empower everyone else's authenticity too. Imagine the freedom to finally be you! It is time, and I know you feel it too.

On your path to authenticity, you will face the three feminine wounds: the bitch wound, the witch wound and the whore wound. You carry them inside. It is said that these wounds originated with Mary Magdalene, who was called a bitch, a witch and a whore. By healing these wounds that have been passed down for centuries, you will live, not just survive, and you will set free all the generations to come.

The Bitch Wound

As women, we naturally tend to take care of everybody before ourselves. Most mothers, overwhelmed by the needs of their kids, husbands, teams, households, friends and parents, are too tired at the end of the day to take care of their own needs. Yet if we dare say "no" to our kids and husbands and put ourselves first, we might very well be called a "bitch."

The bitch takes care of her needs first. The bitch respects herself and knows that she operates best when she is already full—whatever fullness means to her. The bitch fills her cup first before pouring herself into others. Cooking for yourself before cooking for the family, spending an hour in a bath before helping the kids with their homework, rescheduling an appointment with a client to process your own emotions or saying "no" to a family dinner could all earn you the label "bitch."

A woman who respects herself and takes care of her needs first is a very powerful woman. She operates at her best and is literally magnetic. And she scares men. So patriarchal society forces a very negative image on her. But the time for change has arrived. You don't need to fit in to be loved. Taking care of yourself is not self-ish. Saying "no" does not make you a bitch. The belief that we are a bitch if we say "no" has to stop. By saying "no," you set boundaries, you create space for yourself, you put yourself first. And putting yourself first is actually the most generous act. That's how you take care of yourself, elevate your vibration and allow your true light to shine. In that state of being, you can serve others best. There is nothing bitchy about that.

Why not replace "bitch" with "loving and caring woman"?

- If a mother cooks for herself first, she is a loving and caring woman because after filling her cup, she can give her kids all the attention, care and energy they deserve.
- If a woman says "no" to joining a family dinner, she is a loving and caring woman because she knows family drama would drain her and benefit no one.

   o   If a coach reschedules an appointment with a client, she is a loving and caring woman because she knows she can't give her best on that day and will be fully available next time.

Spend some time with Exercise 7 in your **workbook** (see Contents) and journal to let go of the bitch wound.

   o   Where and how do you put others before yourself?
   o   What would you like to say "no" to but don't dare?
   o   What decision will you make today that could be perceived as bitchy? This is your permission to do it and smile at the person who might call you out. It means you succeeded!

Now, go out in the world and be a loving and caring bitch.

The Witch Wound

As women, we have access to mysterious wisdom. We are naturally more intuitive as our cerebellums, the seat of emotions and intuition, are more developed than those of men. Our intuition gives us access to unique pearls of wisdom. This gift scares men who feel like smarter, wiser, mysteriously uncontrollable women take away their power.

A witch is a woman who is connected to her intuition and shows her uniqueness. She knows her intuition is powerful and uses that power in service of the greater good. She serves others with her gifts and wisdom.

The witch wound is the fear of being seen for who you are, being seen for your difference. Because that difference could cost you your life. Historically, women considered witches were burned, tortured and even killed for being different. Though it happened centuries ago in the Western World, women today still carry transgenerational and/or karmic wounds from these times. Your inherited witch wound means being afraid of showing all parts of yourself. Not daring to talk about your work in front of others. Being uncomfortable in front of a camera. Doubting the intuitive messages you receive for others. Keeping to yourself your spiritual experiences unless someone asks you about them. Your witch wound hides that very intuitive, psychic part of yourself because it feels safer to fit in and be like everyone else. Your fear of rejection makes you reject your intuition before anyone else does. Your own rejection feels easier to handle than anyone else's. But by rejecting your own intuition and not sharing your gifts, you actually deny others the expression of theirs. You keep other women in the dark. You prevent them from saying "me too." You dim your lights and theirs without even knowing it.

Why not replace "witch" with "talented woman"?

- Do talented women deserve to be bullied, pushed down or rejected?
- Should talented women hide their talents?
- Can talented women support each other with their unique talents?

You have unique talents. It is your duty to nurture and share them with others, especially those who have yet to connect to their unique talents. Show your natural gifts and express your intuition. Use them to serve with passion, wisdom and care. In doing so, you will truly change lives day after day. You will help others that need your uniqueness, and you will inspire others to do the same. Showing your differences and uniqueness is a generous act. It serves those who need you and heals you at the same time. It breaks the cycle and heals generations of trauma. Help others with your talents and invite them to show their differences too. There is nothing witchy about that.

Return to Exercise 7 in your **workbook** and use the following Ex 7
journaling questions to let go of the witch wound.

- What talent would you share and express if you weren't
  afraid of other people's judgment?
- What part of yourself would you express more if you knew
  you were safe?
- How can you start today?

The Whore Wound

Femininity is tied to being feminine, sensual, desirable, life-
creating and, thus, sexual. Mary Magdalene was considered a
prostitute before she met Jesus. She was called a "whore" and shamed
for it. In reality, she was more of a priestess, a very independent and
sovereign woman who had knowledge of sacred sexuality practices.
But who depicted her as such in history? Nobody of course. Men
recorded history to keep her power and mystic knowledge secret.
In today's world, this whore wound creates much shame around
sensuality and sexuality. Who hasn't been shamed for wearing a
skirt too short or a décolleté too revealing? When men collect
girls or talk about sex for hours, society sees it as normal. But when
women fully assume their sexuality, they are called "whores" and
shamed. We are told that our sensual bodies are dirty and that
our worth, dignity and desirability lie in our purity, our virginity.
"Women who are bedded cannot be wedded."

But how can you be a woman in your power without praising
and honouring the most potent, sacred part of yourself? Intimacy
happens in this sacred part of your body, your womb. It gives you
access to your power and your soul. It is more than a place that
creates life, it is a portal with direct access to Source. You birth
children from this place. But when connecting with your womb,
you also access your most intimate dreams, ideas and projects.

·71·

Sexuality and creativity are really the same energy. Sexual energy is creative energy. They come from the same place: your cosmic womb, your soul.

So, why not replace "whore" with "great creatrix"?

- Does a great creatrix deserve to be shamed for her sensuality and beauty?
- Should a great creatrix hide parts of her creativity for fear of being called names?
- What if we encouraged women to praise their bodies, sexuality and creativity in a respectful and sacred way?
- What if we taught men to control their instincts rather than blaming women for their beauty and power?

Being feminine and subliming your body with nice clothes, jewels, perfume or makeup is a quick and easy way to honour it. You will instantly connect with the infinite creative power within yourself and feel confident, beautiful, powerful. Then when you offer your body to your partner and meet each other in this sacred exchange, you will have a very sacred and spiritual experience. Sexuality is a gift. It connects you with your own power and your partner's power. It holds something very mysterious and mystical. There is absolutely nothing shameful about it.

 Ex 7

Once more, return to Exercise 7 in your **workbook** and use the following journaling questions to let go of the whore wound.

- What parts of your body awaken shame? How can you replace that shame with love?
- List 10 ways you can honour your body.
- Choose one and commit to it for the next 21 days.

Healing and Living in Harmony

"Being inauthentic deprives the Universe of who you came here to be and what you came to express." –Anita Moorjani

On the path of healing and awakening your divine feminine, you unlock the gift of authenticity first. Being authentic with yourself heals the wounded feminine. Only then can you develop the gifts of the integrated, healed feminine who lives in sovereignty.

The wounded feminine negates herself. She is dependent, needy and manipulative because, deep down, she feels disconnected from others and from her power. She longs for oneness, whether that means connection to a partner or belonging to a community. She craves connection because it feels safe and dissolves her fear of rejection. She seeks power outside of herself because she doesn't know she can count on her own inner resources. She adopts the behaviours of a "good girl" in order to be loved and to fit in. She does what others demand and is kind, giving, generous, understanding, not too imposing, not too different and calm. But what society considers a "good girl" is actually a wounded feminine that does not respect herself, depends on others, completes herself through others and is not authentic. We can't judge whether a behaviour is good or bad without considering if it feels right and authentic to ourselves first.

Don't negate who you are or how you feel by trying to behave as a good little girl. To be authentic is to embrace all of yourself, communicate your anger, feel your sadness, show your dissatisfaction, express your boundaries, share your uniqueness, put yourself first. That authenticity heals your wounded feminine and the three feminine wounds. The patriarchy might easily call you a "rebel" or a "selfish bitch" for such behaviour. But actually, you're healing. You're growing spiritually and healing generations of ancestors.

Spiritual growth is not about being nice and negating yourself; it is about embracing the unique, authentic being that you are.

Finally, the gift of authenticity leads to living in harmony, something many of us seek. You might think harmony means being at peace with your environment, your friends, your family. But relationships are often bumpy precisely because they are growth opportunities for both sides.

True harmony is not about being at peace with others, it's being at peace with yourself.

It's about being authentic with yourself. It comes from knowing who you are and why you do certain things. Others won't always understand you. More often than not they won't understand you at all because they haven't walked your path. But it doesn't matter. As long as you understand yourself, your choices, your actions, your words, you will experience harmony. As long as you are authentic, you will live in harmony. When you stop seeking external approval because you know that your internal approval is all that matters, you will embrace your authenticity, heal and walk the path to true sovereignty.

Your Biggest Takeaways from this Gift

....

....

....

....

....

....

....

....

One Action You Choose to Implement Today to Awaken this Gift

....

....

....

....

....

....

....

....

"What you seek is seeking you"

– Rumi

Chapter 7

The Gift of Magnetism

Your Own Fullness

Your body is a magnetic field. Its energy and electricity repel or attract objects, people, situations. Have you ever received a small electric shock when closing a car door? Yes? That's because you have a magnetic field and are magnetic. Your feminine energy, in particular, is naturally magnetic, drawing and repelling. That magnetism can be more or less present, depending on how much you tap into it. Nelson Mandela, Gandhi, Martin Luther King, Jr., Mother Teresa, Amma, Michelle Obama all have something in common: they are magnetic. People absolutely love or hate them. People are drawn or repelled by their energy without really knowing why.

You are magnetic when you are whole and spiritually full of yourself. When your energy is full, you do not need other people's energy to be complete. You don't feed off them. They feel safe around you knowing you won't take their energy away. Your own fullness makes them feel safe and complete, and so they are attracted to you.

You are magnetic when you are *not* trying to convince, manipulate, seduce, please, sell, project, be loved, be needed, be approved. The less you seek, the more you attract and receive because you act from a place of fullness rather than neediness. We all know neediness is unattractive in romantic relationships. Well, it's the same for any relationship. As soon as you interact with another, if you want anything from them, you are less likely to get it. People feel the self-interested intention behind your actions and run away.

It is very human, and completely normal, to act with the hope of a specific result. Actions create outcomes and we tend to believe that there's no result without action. You do certain *things* to get other *things*. You express an argument to convince others that you are right. You give a compliment to be liked. You show up on social media to seduce potential clients. But when you seek a particular result from a particular action, the target feels the energy of neediness and is repelled rather than attracted. Whereas if you act for the simple pleasure of doing it, the right people feel the energy of wholeness and are attracted to you. The intention behind your actions is more potent than any words or arguments you use. The more selfless you are, the more magnetic you are. The more you release attachment, the more magnetic you are. Instead of focusing on the goal, focus on your own fullness, energy and pleasure.

This is an invitation to let go of the old paradigm where you act for a certain outcome. When you don't try to take anything away from others, whether it's love, appreciation, approval, support or money, the right people resonate with your message and actions and are automatically drawn to you. The simple act of being in your fullness and doing things because you simply enjoy doing them makes you completely magnetic. And that's when the magic happens: what is meant for you naturally comes to you.

Grab your downloaded or printed **workbook** (see Contents), and

go through Exercise 8 to confirm you are tapping into your own Ex 8
magnetism today.

The Intention Check

The intention behind your action is always felt. It matters more than any action you take. Even the least psychic or sensitive person feels your intention. We are energy beings. We feel other people's energy whether we are aware of it or not. These energies, or intuition, guide our choices. The more selfless your intention, the more magnetic you are because your intention is the signature of your energy.

So, check in with yourself regularly: "What is my intention behind a particular act?"

By asking yourself this question before going to an interview, a meeting with a potential client, a difficult discussion with a family member or launching a new project, you get clarity on the energy you put out in the world. This energy is what people feel and determines their response.

If you are honest with yourself and do not think your intention is pure, realign and choose to move from selflessness, pleasure and fullness instead. Ask yourself: "How would I feel if I already had this, if it was already done?"

Feel your energy shift and take it from there. If you struggle to change your intention and energy, then ask yourself: "What am I afraid of? Why do I want this so badly? Where in my life do I not feel safe?"

This intention check will guide you to deeper healing and transformation so that you can bring more of that full energy into your life.

Slowing Down

"Nature does not hurry, yet everything is accomplished." –Lao Tzu

Living in cities, being surrounded by concrete, overstimulating our brains, driving cars and eating animals separated us from Nature to the point that we think we control Her. But we are Nature, the source of all things. From Mother Earth we physically came and to Mother Earth we will physically return. Nature even has Her own electromagnetic field, called the Schumann Resonance. When we align with it, we enhance our own magnetism. But this is a challenge for us; the frequencies of the Schumann Resonance move far slower than most humans. Aligning with it feels unnatural since slowing down is one of the greatest challenges of our modern day. We are so used to having everything instantly—instant messaging, instant cooking, instant gratification—that we struggle to wait, to slow down, to give time to time. But Nature needs time, and, by nature, we need it too.

We have been trained to do, control, act, make things happen instead of allowing them to happen. We believe that if we don't do anything, nothing happens. The opposite is actually true. Fia's beautiful song, "The Art of Letting Go," says it all:

The more I struggle and fight
Trying to get it all right
I push away the very thing I want
Thinking it's all up to me
Deciding how it will be
Forgetting that I'm guided by the One
(you can hear here, guided by Nature!)

Pregnancy taught me this very important lesson. I remember wondering: If the Miracle of Life, the perfect creation of a baby, happens naturally without any conscious intervention, why would we need to intervene in order to create our perfect life? Isn't Life also taking care of making everything perfect for each of us?

Let's just pause here and think about babies. The most sophisticated "engine" on Earth, the human body, births perfectly after nine months. It comes when the time is right and is very often a perfect baby. And that all happens on its own without any intervention, effort, control or time pressure.

Why, then, do we feel like we have to battle, struggle and push until exhaustion to bring something to life? Why do we intervene and control so much? Why do we live as if there isn't enough to go around? We want everything right away, quickly, now—expecting it will disappear. We battle, push, struggle, worry, doubt and throw spaghetti against the wall hoping one strand will stick. And it is exhausting. We are drained. We are tired of it.

I believe we have forgotten that Life happens for us, naturally and perfectly, on its own time. We have forgotten that we are magnetic and attract the right people, opportunities, challenges, houses and ideas. Life supports us perfectly, in divine time. The same way it creates a perfect baby that shows up miraculously after nine months.

Pregnancy showed me there was a much better way happening right there, within me. It made me realize that it was time to reconnect to Nature's rhythms. Honour every cycle I was going through. Align to Nature's magnetism. Allow divine timing to happen and create perfection. It's so essential to stop hustling and controlling and start living with trust and a slowness, don't you think?

Richard Rudd, founder of the Gene Keys, has dedicated a whole key to the gift of magnetism. He writes in his book, *The Gene Keys*, that "Since magnetism is the binding force of all creatures and forms, the more deeply you move into the Schumann Resonance, the more magnetic you become. This is all about trusting the natural ebb and flow of life events.... To live closely to the Earth's natural rhythms is to experience the wisdom and clarity that comes of moving more slowly through the world." These few sentences emphasize how trust in Nature's timing and slowing down are key to becoming magnetic. So go out, have a walk, observe Nature's rhythms and invite them into your life.

You can also move into the Schumann Resonance by consciously shifting into alpha brain waves (8 to 12 Hertz). Your brain is naturally in alpha mode when you first wake up in the morning. Why not stay in bed a little longer and enjoy this natural state of relaxation? Meditation and daydreaming also boost alpha brain waves. Dedicated music and brain waves apps also stimulate alpha waves in the brain. Introduce these activities in your everyday life, and your auric field will naturally become more magnetic. It is as simple as that: slow down, meditate, daydream, go for a walk and the things that are meant for you will come to you. Too simple to be true? Try it out and let me know how it goes!

Walking Down the Aisle

There's nothing more magnetic than a beautiful, confident bride walking down the aisle. She embodies trust in the unknown, slowing down and pure attraction. Every single person in the room looks at her. She draws all the attention. Some might love or hate her attire. Some might want to be by her side, hug her, kiss her or hold her, yet she is inaccessible in that moment, making her even more desirable. She walks slowly. She knows she has time. Everyone is there for her. There's no reason to rush. She shines. The wholeness, love and joy she feels in that moment shines through the power of her aura. She is absolutely magnetic.

The bride that draws a lot of attention is the kind of energy you want to carry in your life. There are four main practical aspects of this magnetic embodiment.

○ Self-care: "I love myself and take great care of myself."
The day a bride gets married, she spends several hours devoted to making herself feel confident and stunning. Likewise, when you spend time honouring yourself on a simple weekday by taking care of your appearance, you enhance your mood and how you feel about yourself. You feel more assured and send a very clear message to the world: I love myself and I take care of myself. This message of self-love is magnetic and draws attention. Leave the house feeling replenished and confident, and with a sense of self-care and self-love. It is not about the style of your appearance; it is about how it makes you feel to take care of yourself. That energy will be felt by every person you talk to and will draw even more love and attention.

○ Faith: "I do."
When a bride gets married, she says "I do" to someone for the rest of her life. She doesn't know what the future holds, but she believes she and her spouse can face the storms and sunny days together. That trust is magnetic. What if you believe in your future as strongly as a bride who says "Yes" to the love of her life? You know you're about to make a life-changing decision, but you still go for it. When you think about it, every decision you make every day can be life-changing in the long run. The food you eat, the person you date, the new client you sign, the coach you invest in, the conversation you have. . . . They feel like small decisions compared to a marriage, but they have huge ripple effects. Believe in yourself, believe in your future and trust that every decision you make is what you need in that precise moment.

○   Presence: "I savour every moment."
When a bride walks down the aisle, she walks slowly. She wants to take in every second of that day. Even though she might be carried away by the emotional roller coaster, she does her best to savour every moment. She is present. She slows down. She takes her time. Because she knows that every second she experiences is a second less of that magical day. Why would it be different any other day? Life is precious and every second you experience is a second that will never come back. You live it, and then it's gone. Like a bride, pause for a moment in your days, slow down, look around, and take in the beauty of that moment. Savour it.

○   Inaccessibility: "I put myself first."
The day a bride gets married is pretty busy! Everybody wants a part of her or at least a hug and a selfie with her. She's happy to share that joy with everyone, but she also puts her desires first. If she finds herself stuck with an old uncle that has had too much champagne, she won't hesitate to excuse herself and find some friends to hang out with, right? It's her day after all! Well, every day can be like that day! Every day is your day. Every day is an opportunity to put yourself first. Every day is an opportunity to devote yourself to your passions, hobbies and interests. Your life is much more colourful and enjoyable, and you're a happier person. You're also a busier person and less available for others, which makes you more attractive. By putting yourself first and making your desires and passions your priority, you become happier, busier and more magnetic.

What if you walked the aisle of your life as a bride walks down her wedding aisle every day—feeling stunning, loved, desired, taking the leap, trusting the unknown, walking very slowly to the love of your life?

Whenever you are about to do something that matters, connect to that magnetic bridal feeling. Close your eyes, see yourself feeling amazing, walking very slowly to your partner who's looking at you with infinite love, ready to take the leap with you, trusting the unknown of your future life together. Feel that love, trust and magnetism in your whole body. Feel how empowering, whole and safe it is. Then, in that energy, take action. Walk on the stage, jump on the sales call, go to the interview, send the email, speak from your heart. All is well. You are supported and loved. You are magnetic. Everything that is meant for you is on its way to you.

Longing versus Needing

Before having a look at these two emotions, we must agree on their definition. What is "longing" to you? Per the dictionary, a longing is "a strong, persistent desire for something distant or unattainable."

Let's consider that a desire might be distant or unattainable. There's a notion of lack and frustration here, right? But let's remember that our inner feminine is receptive. It is not her role to take the first action. Her role is to identify what she wants and then let the masculine deliver it. A longing, then, is a strong desire that becomes absolutely attainable when you are in sacred union, working in harmony with your active, masculine energy. So, I define longing as "a desire for something coming from a place of fullness, of hope, of dreams," rather than a place of lack.

When you act from that place of longing, you are magnetic. In your business, for example, your desire to share your gifts fills someone else's need. You attract those you can serve and who resonate with your energy of fullness.

Furthermore, this notion of fullness, of love, is very important because it helps you identify whether your desire is aligned. Whether it's a longing coming from your divine feminine or not. If the desire comes from a place of lack, of neediness, it is not aligned. It is a need probably coming from your wounded feminine or masculine. A "needing" behind your actions creates misalignment, chaos and exhaustion in your life. The longing behind your actions brings success, ease, and pleasure. Let's compare the two.

I want a baby because I want to raise a family and experience that joy.
I want a baby because I need a purpose in my life.

I want a partner in order to grow together and have fun.
I want a partner in order to feel safe and complete.

I want to have sex because I enjoy the intimacy and connection experienced with my partner.
I want to have sex because I need to feel desired, beautiful, loved. . . .

I want to help women because I want to make an impact and support them with struggles I know about.
I want to help women because I need to feel useful, important, seen. . . .

Can you sense the difference between these two? Can you feel the different energy you put out when you long for something versus need something?

Longing is a pure feminine energy. Your inner feminine is there to help you identify what you truly desire. She decides what she wants, hopes, dreams of. And then the masculine sets up the structure and foundation necessary to create this vision. When you long for something, you connect to your divine feminine. You open the field of possibilities, visualizing it, dreaming it, feeling it, already enjoying it while your whole body is turned on by the idea of your desire coming true. That excitement comes directly from your gut, your sacral, your womb space; it is the divine feminine's way of telling you something is right for you. It is aligned. It is your soul showing you the way. And when you follow the way, you magnetize your desire to you.

The masculine then steps up. The masculine can be another part of yourself, the Universe or the dream client you magnetize by connecting with your longing. He's grateful to know what to do next and will do his best to provide. He plans, structures, executes and delivers. He honours, respects and supports the feminine and wants her to feel safe and loved. He feels complete by bringing her what she wants and making her happy.

The feminine finally births the idea into matter; she creates thanks to the support, structure, foundation and tools brought by the masculine. As women, we are here to create. Our wombs, our whole feminine energy, long to create. We create, shed, birth, then retreat, and create, shed and birth again. We go in cycles. We're naturally creative and our inner masculine brings the structure and the action that allows the creativity to become a real project.

This process happening within you is a sacred dance between your masculine and your feminine. The energy flows from one to the other with ease. The feminine longs and desires and the masculine structures and provides. She guides the dance and receives from him. She's playful, he supports her. She dreams, he makes it concrete. She asks, he delivers. She's grounded, he anchors her more. She savours pleasure, he brings her more of it. Even physically, we are built like that. In the sexual exchange, women receive. We open ourselves to our partners, they penetrate us.

For this sacred union and magnetism to exist within you, both energies need to meet with innocence. This innocence is a true openness to receive the other. To listen. To care. To let go of any judgment. It is what bonds the two energies with respect, forgiveness, safety, trust, patience, gratitude and devotion. This innocence creates a strong, stable, limitless sacred union within you. The creative process of Life can then take place and inevitably lead to success.

To create sacred union with innocence and then create from a place of fullness, you need self-awareness and integrity. Only you know what happens inside. Only you have access to your inner world. When you feel a desire, pay close attention to its root and ask yourself in full honesty and without any judgment:

- Is this a longing or a needing?
- Why do I really want this? What's the root of this desire?
- What will it bring me? What do I do this for?

Is it based on authentic excitement because you feel joyful about experiencing this desire or are you excited because this desire feels like answering a need for security, a need to prove yourself or a need to be loved and seen?

The root of your desire, the root of your excitement, has to be selfless for it to be magnetic. Your divine feminine has nothing to prove. She IS and knows that being is more than enough.

Ask yourself if that is true for you right now. Do you know that you are more than enough? Do you feel in your bones that your unique presence makes a difference in the world, and that there is nothing else you need to do? Your vibration, your frequency, is more than enough. Whether you keep that to yourself by living in a lonely hut or share that vibration with friends, family, clients, sports teams. . . . We are all connected, so you impact others and the Earth itself just by being you in your highest vibration. That's what the feminine is meant to do; *being* in her highest vibe. That's all.

In 2018, I was living in Montreal, studying energy healing and healing myself from my recent divorce. One morning, I got up from a dream and said to myself: "Healing works like a spiral and it has six steps. It's a self-healing spiral!" I jumped out of bed, sat behind my laptop and drew the six steps. Then I thought: "I *need* to share this with other women, I *need* to write a book!"

I felt a need to share my story. It took me two years to see that I was answering a need to be seen, to be useful and to have a project that could financially support me. My future was uncertain, and I believed a book sharing "the self-healing spiral" could help me rebuild my life. So, when this method came to me, it felt like I'd found the Holy Grail. I felt like I had won the lottery. I was overwhelmed with excitement. But mostly, I suddenly felt safe. That same day, I wrote the table of contents and began the book. Chapter after chapter, day after day, from 9:00 am to 6:00 pm, I wrote. I finished it in eight weeks and then took another few months to improve it. It was a very pushy, structured, rational, excited but needy, wounded feminine and masculine approach.

In hindsight, I smile thinking about this girl that was pushing mountains to get what she wanted. That's where self-awareness plays an important role. By checking in with your intention, you gain clarity about yourself and discover from which place you're taking action. But I didn't know that at the time. My intention was to have a project, to make a difference—in order to feel important. My *need* to share that book made me feel safe. I wrote the book in French, published it, translated it into English and dreamt of building a foundation to teach the method to kids all over the world. I felt inspired … but mostly I felt safe and confident that I had proven myself. I didn't know I was already safe and had nothing to prove.

Remember, neediness comes from the wounded feminine. My need to be seen and feel safe came from my wounded feminine that believed I wasn't good enough and lived in the illusion that I wasn't safe. Once the excitement of publishing the book in French and in English was over, that project stopped feeling aligned. The excitement about teaching the method faded away when the need to prove myself and to feel safe disappeared…. I realized it was a chapter I had to experience but not the happy ending I expected. A new, more aligned chapter made of longings rather than needs then started for me.

In 2020, when I had the idea to write this book you're holding in your hands, I was in a meditation and thought, "It would be fun to write a book about the divine feminine and support women on this quest." It felt exciting, fun and joyful. I remember feeling chills all over my body. I got out of my meditation and shared my new desire with my husband. The next day, I again reflected on the idea to see how I felt about it. And on that day, I still wanted to write a book, so I sat behind my laptop and randomly wrote about a story I remembered. Then I wrote a few ideas for later and left it there. I waited another week to write about this chapter and understood this new project came from a healed place, a place of fullness. I left the book again for a few days until I woke up in the middle of the night and received more guidance from my spirit squad, which is what I shared in the Introduction.

This creative process was a very different experience than writing my first book. I would only write when the inspiration came, *and* I felt excited about it. No fixed days or hours. No pressure or structure. I wrote with the intention of enjoying the process itself and sharing my thoughts and experiences with the hope that it might resonate with other women. There was no neediness, only longing to do something I have always enjoyed: writing and sharing. Knowing that I could help women on this topic without writing a book—via speaking gigs, podcasts, social media, coaching and energy healing sessions—indicated that there was no *need* for me to write a book to share this message. Instead, I birthed this book only because of the pleasure it brought me to write and to spend hours doing that on a Friday evening, Sunday afternoon or Tuesday lunch break.

In the end, it took me five months to write this book, compared to the eight weeks for my first book, *The Self-Healing Spiral*. It was still a very quick process, but it felt easy and effortless. I was in flow. Instead of running after time, I ran after enjoyment in the present moment. The result was the same: I wrote a book. But the intention and process came from longing, not needing; and, thus, I magnetized its completion. I didn't need to seek a publisher; I magnetized one that was introduced to me. I didn't need to look for cover art; the artist simply offered to do it when I told her about my book. I am curious to witness what else I will attract when all of you, my readers, have this book in your hands.

This difference of intention, longing versus needing, is how you know if an action is aligned or misaligned. It's the difference between an easy and successful project or one that is hard and draining. Remember, if you long for something, without needing it at all, your divine feminine is showing you the way of joy, abundance, alignment and fun, which, in turn, means that you will magnetize its success. It is more than ok to have longings; they are necessary in order to have an aligned life! But if there's a slight need in your vision or desire, check again later and ask yourself: "What do I really long for and why do I really want this?"

Your Biggest Takeaways from this Gift

....

....

....

....

....

....

....

One Action You Choose to Implement Today to Awaken this Gift

....

....

....

....

....

....

....

"In the space of no-mind, truth descends like light."

—Osho

Chapter 8

The Gift of Intuition

Your Intuition Is Your Soul's Language

You speak with words and sounds, right? You also speak with your body. Your eyes, facial expressions and arm positions help communicate desires and feelings. Your whole body expresses itself toward the outside world. This nonverbal, subconscious communication completes, supports and specifies what you try to say with simple words. It is an external communication from your body to the world.

Your body also has an internal communication: your intuition. Coming from another part of yourself, called your soul, higher self or eternal self, this language is also expressed through your body but directed to your inner world. It is meant to be understood by only you. You have a powerful intuition that's constantly communicating with you. There's no such thing as a bad intuition. Your intuition is always talking to you. But you have to learn to listen and interpret this other kind of nonverbal communication.

Nonverbal communication is innate. A baby does not need to learn to smile to express its happiness. It does not need to learn to cry to show its frustration or needs. It does so naturally. The recipient of the communication, however, must learn to interpret the baby's nonverbal communication. Your intuition works the same way. You do not need to learn to express your soul's wisdom; it expresses itself naturally. But you need to learn to understand your intuition—to listen and then interpret it. Like every language, it can be daunting and frustrating at first, but once mastered, it opens the doors of a whole new world.

Learning intuition is trickier than other nonverbal languages, however, because there's no teacher. Your intuition comes from you and is directed to you, so no one else can interpret it. You are the teacher and the student here. You must learn it on your own with patience, experience and trust.

Nonetheless, many spiritual teachers, shamans and psychics have shared their experiences and teachings in order to make this inner school easier for you. Before diving deeper into the different ways your intuition talks to you, you need to first understand the differences between your ego and your soul. They are both part of you and express themselves to you. By distinguishing them and understanding their differences, you know exactly which is speaking to you. This will help you create space to better hear your intuition.

Ego versus Soul: How to Differentiate Them

Often ego is considered a part of you that is overly proud. Someone with a big ego might talk about herself a lot and take up space in the room. But that's a very limiting connotation of ego. Your ego is the sum of your roles, masks, identities and experiences. It is a beautiful little guardian that has one main goal:

keeping you safe. And it comes up with plenty of strategies to fulfill its purposes: ensuring that you have as much love as possible and don't take too many risks. The ego keeps you safe due to its fear of death. But this deeply rooted fear then surfaces disguised as other fears, such as fear of rejection or abandonment, or fears of suffering, struggling or being uncomfortable, and turns into needs, such as the need to be loved, to fit in, to be protected or to stay safe.

Because the ego fights for survival while the soul is eternal and, thus, limited by this fear, many spiritual teachers talk about killing the ego in order to allow the soul to come through. And while I understand this idea, I truly believe that the ego should not be killed. On the contrary, the ego must be loved.

If you tell a crying toddler—or even a crying adult—to stop crying, they will cry harder. If you ask a crying toddler what's wrong and give them validation and love, they feel understood, stop crying and move on. Your ego is a toddler crying for attention and love. And that's truly all it needs to slow down, relax and move on.

Your ego was created in your psyche around the age of 2 or 3 and has since then fulfilled its purpose of keeping you safe. It created beliefs, masks, worries, fears, protections and roles to fulfill its purpose. And thank God it did, otherwise you probably wouldn't have survived until today. Your ego was necessary for your survival. But like every survival mechanism, it is fear-based, a child's strategy that no longer fits into an adult's world. Be grateful for everything it allowed you to experience but recognize that it does not fit the adult world you are now part of.

Healing yourself means healing your ego and letting go of beliefs, fears and masks that don't fit anymore and prevent you from fulfilling your soul's purpose. Because your soul also has a purpose! A unique purpose that is completely different from your ego's purpose. One is focused on keeping you safe; it is restricting. The other has to do with sharing your uniqueness with the world; it is expansive. You have to let go of the first to let the second unfold. So, this is your time to decide: Do you keep fulfilling your ego's purpose or do you move on to finding your soul's purpose?

I assume you are ready to move on, willing to let go of all the old habits that do not serve you anymore and open to understanding your soul's language, your intuition, which leads you on the path of finding your true purpose. Right? Well, where do you start? First, understand who your ego is and how it acts so that you can identify when he's taking the lead.

Let me present to you your ego.

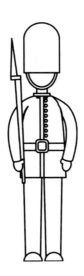

His name: ………………………….. Give him a cute, endearing name that will bring a smile to your face. Remember, love, do not kill, the ego.
Size: Tall and imposing.
Outfit: Guardian attire, ready to fight for survival.

Characteristics:

- o Competitive; believes there's not enough to go around for everyone.
- o Fearful; makes fear-based decisions.
- o Judgmental; believes everything is either good or bad.
- o Doubtful; wonders if he's good enough.
- o Arrogant; sometimes believes he's better than anyone else.
- o Lonely; doesn't feel connected to anyone; lives in separation.
- o Creative; comes up with many meanings about people's behaviours.
- o Time traveler; always thinks about the future or the past.
- o Stubborn; will never let go of wanting to keep you safe. Never.
- o Picky Prince; really, really doesn't like to be uncomfortable.

Other aspects:

- o His main needs are to be heard, seen and loved.
- o Talks in an assertive, directive way, using "you."
- o Expresses himself through your thoughts and emotions.
- o Creates beliefs, masks, roles, identities, meanings, assumptions and fears.

Love and thank your ego, your little guardian, for all the hard work that he has done to keep you safe all these years. He's been devoted to you, and he never stopped doing his best. When your ego is fearful—when you are fearful—go within and have a little chat with this part of yourself. Reassure yourself, give yourself validation for whatever you feel and take the time to feel whatever is asked to be felt. Then connect with a moment where you felt loved. Doing this consistently lowers the power of your ego and creates space for your soul to come through.

Here's a short exercise to help you connect with your ego and give him the love and reassurances he needs—give yourself the reassurances and love you need. You can access the audio version

Ex 9 of this visualization by clicking the link at Exercise 9 in your **workbook** (see Contents). I invite you to do this visualization as it is very potent.

Master Your Little Guardian

1. Close your eyes and think about something that could go wrong in your life, something that worries you, a fear you have. Allow yourself to really think about it and feel the fear spread through your body.
2. Identify where this fear resides in your body and put your hand there.
3. Then visualise this fear:
    - Is it a man or a woman?
    - How old is it?
    - How is it dressed?
4. Get closer to your fear and, with much compassion, talk to it. Say the following or use your own words to reassure it:
    "Thank you, my little guardian. *Thank you for keeping me safe.* I know you've been here for a long time, doing this hard work and I'm grateful for it. But I want you to know that I am safe. It's ok to be afraid. It's ok to be worried. But everything is fine at this present moment. Everything is fine right now. You don't need you to protect me any-more. You can let go. Whatever happens in the future, I have everything within me to take care of it. I take full responsibility for the future. Everything is fine. Everything will be fine. Thank you so much for your love and care all these years. I love you. Goodbye."
5. Inhale and exhale deeply through your nose and bring your awareness back to the room you are in.

Identifying when your ego is talking to you helps you give him what he needs: love and healing. By doing so, you realize that you

·100·

are not these thoughts in your mind. You are not the fear that's holding you back from quitting your job to follow your dreams. You are not this exuberant laugh that is trying to attract the attention of the handsome individual sitting across the room. You are not the sarcastic voice that is pushing a relative down. You are much more than that.

"Don't believe everything you think." –Allan Lokos

The more you practice this exercise, validate your emotions, reassure your ego and shed the habits that don't work anymore, the more you let go of this fake identity. You then create space for your soul, your authentic self, to come through. Your soul needs silence, tranquility, openness, flow and fun to express itself.

Now that you've met your ego, it's time to meet your soul. Well, what is your soul, and how does it present itself? Here's a short introduction:

Her name: .... Your soul's name holds a unique vibration that says something about your purpose. A healer, medium or psychic could identify her.

Size: Infinitely big and expansive.
Outfit: None and does not need any.
Characteristics:

- Expansive; always expanding and looking for growth, evolution.
- Eternal; never dies, no fear of death.
- In the present moment; does not think about tomorrow or yesterday.
- One; connected to all things and all people.
- All-knowing; knows what's best for you and where you need to go; isn't wedded to the idea of time and space.
- Suggestive; makes suggestions and allows you to listen or not.
- Nonjudgmental; does not judge others or the ego in any way.
- Peaceful; at ease, deeply relaxed in every situation.
- Talks in words, suggestions, colours, images, feelings and sensations.

By knowing the main characteristics of your ego and soul, you can easily identify "who" is talking to you. If the talk is fear-based or judgmental, your ego is expressing itself and needing attention. If the talk is loving and suggestive, your soul is guiding you in a new direction.

The way your body experiences both types of thoughts is also very different. Your ego feels restrictive, whereas your soul feels expansive. You can feel both at the same time—an idea's expansiveness and the ego's fear. It is actually a good sign if you feel both at the same time. It's your soul bringing you somewhere your ego does not know, out of your comfort zone, where growth and expansion lie. And that's definitely a scary place for your ego. Fear then becomes a sign that you are going in the right direction—the direction of listening to your intuition and soul.

Three Ways Your Intuition Talks

Your intuition expresses itself in three different ways through your body: you can hear, see or feel it. You might be more comfortable already with one of these and use that channel even without noticing it. But you can also develop the two others with time, practice and trust.

When you hear your intuition, you might expect to hear another, different voice in your head, as if it was coming from outside of yourself. But really, you'll hear your own voice. It is YOUR intuition. So, it is YOUR voice. How do you differentiate it from the other voices in your head like the tyrant, the not-good-enough voice or the inner child? Well, it is actually quite simple. Your intuition has another vibration. It speaks completely differently than the various voices of your ego. Let's have a look at these differences.

First, your soul suggests ideas, directions and choices. It never demands anything. You have free will, remember? So, your intuition is suggestive: "What if I…?" "Shall I …?" "I could…?" Your ego, on the other hand, is insistent and uses the word "should." "You should do this, that, go there, sign up for this…." Your pushy ego forces you in one direction.

Because your soul lives in the present moment and is connected to all moments as one, it suggests small, random actions to take in the present moment. It does not present a clear vision or explain the why behind the suggestion. It simply suggests that you get this book, listen to this podcast, go to that party, sit on that side of the table, etc. You might not know why you feel like doing something so random in the moment, but your soul, who's connected to all moments, knows.

Your ego is the opposite. It focuses on the past or the future and likes to imagine long-term worst-case scenarios. It talks about the consequences of your actions and justifies why you should or should not do something in the future or should have done or not done something in the past. On top of that, your ego's messages are usually filled with fear and judgment. "I shouldn't have said that. Now, they are all going to hate me." "I should write a blog if I want clients to sign up for my program." "I'm not good enough, that's why he dumped me."

Additionally, your intuition talks in the first person. Picture gifting yourself a new outfit. You write on the gift card: "From me to me," right? Likewise, your intuition comes from you, your higher self, and is directed to you. So, your intuition says: "What if I went right?" "What if I bought this book?" "Shall I stay home today?" Your ego, on the other hand, mostly talks in the second person: "You're so stupid, why did you do that?" "You're a badass, well done!" "You should get up rather than staying in bed!" But ego is tricky. It sometimes also talks in the first person: "I'm not good enough...."

An extra way to differentiate intuition from ego is to observe the tone of the voice in your head. Your intuition is loving and all-knowing. It has your highest good at heart. Your intuition always suggests simple, loving actions that will lead you to more. Your ego has a very bossy, worried tone. It is a little schizophrenic and dramatic. One day, it says: "Who do you think you are? Nobody cares about your work/book/movie/song/project. You're not good enough." The next day, it says: "See, everybody loves your work. Well done! You're awesome! You're the best!"

Finally, your intuition expresses itself very quickly and very subtly. It suggests something in the fraction of a second, almost at the speed of light. Sometimes you only hear a word instead of a sentence. You need to be calm, centred, grounded to hear it. If you're too busy thinking, worrying or wondering, you could easily miss it. Your ego, on the other hand, likes to insist. It repeats what it said five minutes ago, will probably repeat it again later and could talk about the same thing for hours. Your ego sounds like a scratched record, for those of you who still listen to records. And your soul sounds like a feather in the wind.

In a nutshell, it is your intuition talking when you hear your own voice suggest something simple—a random action—in a loving, subtle, quick way, with a word or a sentence starting like this: "What if…?" "Shall I…?" "I could…?"

	SOUL	EGO
CONTENT	Suggestions	Firm requests or judgments
CONTENT	Random, small actions	Actions with long-term consequences
TIME-FOCUS	Present moment	Future or past
TONE	Loving, all-knowing	Bossy, dramatic, fear-based
SPEED	Subtle, quick, flowy like a feather in the wind	Repetitive, insistent like a scratched record
USE OF PERSON	1st person: "I"	1st or 2nd person: "I" or "You"
WORDING	Shall I…, What if…, I could…	You/I should…, I am…

Seeing is another channel for your intuition, one that invites you to exercise the trust muscle. When you first see a vision, your reaction might be something like: "It's my imagination." "I'm making this up." Or "It's not real." Right? That's because you have not learned to trust your imagination, which has been pushed down by our rational, logical, left-brained society. But what if your imagination is the very thing connecting you to your intuition? What if your intuition uses your imagination to deliver messages to you? When you dream, you see images coming from your inner eye. Do these dreams have no messages for you? Of course they do. Your dreams have plenty of messages for you, just like your imagination does. If you see something in your mind's eye, it is your soul using these images to talk to you.

Learn to trust what you see. The human eye only sees 2 percent of reality. You might as well see nothing, that's how close you are to being blind. What if your imagination covers part of the other 98 percent of reality? Suddenly, your imagination would make a lot of sense, right? Well, it does. Trust what you see when you close your eyes, and you will receive even more guidance. You can always double-check what you see by asking your body how it feels about this inner vision. Your body never lies.

Feeling is my main channel and my favourite way to connect with my intuition. Most women have this channel, along with hearing or seeing to accentuate it. Our bodies use sensations and feelings to guide us. Something feels expansive or restrictive. Warm or cold. Open or closed.

Your intuition is always available to you, so you can use this channel on demand by simply by tuning in to your body. Slow down your breathing, go into your heart or your womb and ask, "How does this feel to me?" You can do this all day long to check for messages.

Do a quick body scan, observe where there's tension and ask yourself where that tension comes from and what it has to say.

How often do you listen to your body?

How often do you sit in silence to listen to your inner world and tune in with the wisdom of your body?

The more you are in tune with your body, the more you strengthen that communication channel. Eventually, it will become very easy for you to make decisions based on your intuition and what you feel.

Now that you have a better understanding of how your intuition speaks to you, learn to interpret it. Practice. Don't be afraid to fail. You can't fail at this game, actually. It's a learning process that has plenty of gifts and rewards waiting for you along the path.

Day after day, your mind will feel more at ease with your intuition until the day it feels comfortable enough to give your soul the lead. Because your mind is of service to your soul. This powerful machine inside your skull is there to serve your soul's desires. It has its own desires, for sure. But with time, all the voices in your head will seem smaller, almost absent, and your intuition will come through consistently. That's when your soul guides your life, and everything unfolds naturally, magically, for your highest good.

An Inner GPS

In November 2018, I was in Los Angeles visiting my then boyfriend, now husband. He worked during the day, so I had a few free hours to explore the city. I decided to do a movie-tour that would take me through Beverly Hills to the public art sculpture, "Urban Light." This large-scale assemblage of lanterns, located in front of the Los

Angeles County Museum of Art, is home to many romantic movie scenes. My cheesy heart definitely wanted to check it out!

Coming from Santa Monica, it would be easy to find Beverly Hills. Driving to the museum, on the other hand, would require guidance. I put the address in Google Maps, and hit the road hoping the GPS would stay on, even though I had no data due to my phone being based in Quebec. I lost the GPS connection as soon as I left the flat and moved away from its Wi-Fi. I tried to connect to the city Wi-Fi, but that didn't work either. I was in a good mood, chose not to worry and focused on my first destination—the fancy houses surrounded by palm trees of Beverly Hills. It was quite easy to get there, and I was really enjoying myself. Taken away by the beauty of the neighbourhood, I quickly forgot I was in one of the biggest cities of the world, without a map!

Reality caught up when I was done driving around Sunset Boulevard. I stopped the car on the side of the road and tried again to connect to the city Wi-Fi. No success. I kept driving, bringing myself closer and closer to the center of L.A. I again stopped and tried to connect to any Wi-Fi my phone would find. And again, it failed. I zoomed in on the map to try to find the museum somewhere in the middle of all those streets. That's when I realized how big L.A. is! I obviously never found it. There I was, with a destination in mind, but no idea how to find it or get there. I had tried to rely on my friend, Wi-Fi, but he wasn't very reliable on that day! So, I had nothing left to trust but myself. I thought, "Oh well, how terrible can it be to drive around a city for a few hours and just go with the flow?" I decided to have fun and kept driving around. With no destination in mind anymore, I was just going right, left and following the little hints I would feel in my body: "What if I turned right here?" "There seems to be a nice street there, let's check it out." "That looks like a nice building over there, let's drive to it." After 30 minutes of going with the flow, I saw a big building with red light and lots of cars turning left in front of it. I thought, "What if I follow the cars?" So, I did. I drove a few more meters and suddenly started laughing hysterically. I was just in front of the Los Angeles County Museum of Art. Immediately to my left was the beautiful public art installation, "Urban Light." I could not believe it. How did I manage to end up exactly where I wanted, without any map, in the middle of this huge city? I was in total awe of what had just happened. It blew my mind. My intuition had brought me exactly where I wanted to be, and I got there just by following the hints of my body. No pressure from my mind, just flow and fun. That day, I realized my all-knowing intuition was probably the most trustworthy GPS in the world.

Your inner GPS always knows the best way to get you where you want.

Your intuition, the language of your Soul, also directly connects you to Source. When your intuition guides your life, you are a channel for Life. You allow Life itself to work through you, for your highest good and the highest good of others.

I want to help you lead your life more with your intuition. Do Exercise 10, the Heart-Brain Coherence, in your **workbook** (see Contents) to connect with this all-knowing, always available guidance. These following five steps have been studied and assembled by the HeartMath® Institute for deeper connection with your soul.

1. Focus on your heart. Allow your awareness to move from your mind to the heart area.
   - This sends a signal to your heart that a shift has occurred. Become aware of the world within you rather than the world around you.
2. Slow your breathing. Take six-second inhales and six-second exhales.

- This sends a signal to your body that you are safe and in a supportive place. This also stimulates the relaxation response of the parasympathetic nervous system.

3. Feel rejuvenated. Feel a genuine sense of care, gratitude, appreciation, love and compassion for anything or anyone.
   - The quality of this feeling fine tunes and optimizes the coherence between the brain and the heart.

4. Ask your heart a question. It doesn't need context, situations or details. Ask a simple and straight-to-the-point question.
   - "From the place of my heart's deepest knowing, I ask to be shown the significance of..."
   - "Is it right for me to..."
   - "Please, help me understand the significance of..."

5. Listen for an answer. Feel the sensations your body sends you. Images, colours, words, warmth.... Don't try to make sense of the sensations at first, just allow them to be and integrate them.

Your Biggest Takeaways from this Gift

....

....

....

....

....

....

....

....

One Action You Choose to Implement Today to Awaken this Gift

....

....

....

....

....

....

....

"My formula for success was very simple: Do whatever is put in front of you with all your heart and soul without regard for personal results. Do the work as though it were given to you by the universe itself—because it was."

—Michael Singer

Chapter 9

The Gift of Surrender

Does "surrendering" sound like a counterintuitive way of living? In a culture that is go-go-go, where big companies' slogans invite us to "Just do it," burnout is worn like a badge of honour. We're expected to work hard and play hard, and rest seems to be limited to the 8 to 20 paid holidays we receive. In that context, surrender is definitely seen as a weird, inadequate, woo-woo concept. It is associated with not getting results, being lazy and waiting for success to fall from the sky. Too often, "surrenderers" are maligned as either hippies living in a van or losers that won't ever get anywhere. But what if people are wrong about the concept of surrender? What if surrender is the missing element to getting what you want? What if it holds a gift you don't even know you need?

The divine feminine surrenders. She accepts what is and allows things to unfold and come to her. She co-creates her life and relies on that invisible force to guide her and make things happen for her. She expresses her desires, shares her vision, and then allows her co-creator to take the masculine role and bring her what she wants. She trusts. She doesn't control. She stays in her feminine energy until she feels her intuition lead her to the right next aligned action. Then she invites the divine masculine, the do-er, to take action.

Many people understand surrendering as letting go. Actually, it has nothing to do with letting go. Rather, surrender is about letting things go their natural way. Letting things unfold naturally without forcing any outcome. Trusting that no matter the path, you will get where you need to be. Like the river that finds her way into the ocean, she goes right and left, up and down. She follows the path of ease and gets to the ocean with a smile on her drops. She does not go in a straight line to the ocean, overriding the hills, rushing through the fields and fighting all sorts of resistance. The river moves naturally and gets where she needs to, effortlessly.

For you, beautiful human being who wants to let go of control and surrender to Life like the river surrenders to her environment, you have to accept and embrace what is instead of fighting and resisting what is. Embrace the trigger, embrace the rejection, embrace the redirection, embrace the obstacles. And follow the emotion, follow the flow, follow the ease, follow the signs. Simply put, you are invited to follow the path of the least resistance and trust what's coming your way.

Surrender doesn't mean you lay on your couch all day and wait. It's not inactivity or inertness. Rather, surrender takes a passive action of acceptance and trust. Not making a decision is still making a decision. Not taking action is still acting. My husband once said to me, "Your heart beats half of the time and rests half the time. Still, you are fully alive, and everything is done." Sometimes, doing nothing and allowing Life to unfold is the best act. When it really is time to take concrete action, your intuition shows you the way; you simply surrender to the guidance you receive. Trust the sudden idea, the desire coming from your body, the warmth in your sacral, the feeling of expansiveness, the surprising vision,

THE GIFT OF SURRENDER

the out-of-the-blue song on the radio, the bird knocking on the window, the curious invitation to join a social media group or the book someone tells you about. Signs are everywhere. Guidance is everywhere. You need to be in a receptive, still, surrendered state to be able to perceive them.

The Power of Uncertainty

In the first chaotic months of 2020, I wondered what surrender really meant for my life. I wanted to flow like a river and reach my ocean with a smile on my face, not more wrinkles around my eyes. I chose to let things go their natural way. I chose to stop hustling, worrying, pushing. I accepted resistance as a gift. I saw rejections as redirections and learned to be grateful every time someone said "no." I trusted something else would show up. I sat more in silence. I allowed myself to be more creative and to have more fun. I embraced all the space and doubt that surrender created in my life. In the midst of this experience, I recognized how hard it was to surrender. Because it meant facing the uncertainty of life. Not knowing what tomorrow held. Not knowing which direction things could go. Not knowing what was about to come. Letting go of expectations and attachment. Taking risks. Living with risks. Imagining the worst. Not controlling outcomes. Not controlling people. Not controlling at all. But, instead, embracing and surrendering to the uncertainty of tomorrow and the next weeks, months and years. The remainder of 2020 forced upon us a lot of uncertainty with its human health crisis. What better opportunity to learn to surrender?

My ego constantly created fear around uncertainty. Once I overcame that fear, I had a breakthrough. I realized that by approaching my days and weeks without knowing what they would hold, I created space for surprising events to unfold. I realized that uncertainty held magic. I had no expectations, so

I could only be surprised. Some surprises were good, others less so. But I was experimenting with surrender, so I let go of my resistance when facing disappointments and chose to believe something better would come instead. These particular disappointments taught me that I still maintained expectations and hoped to see things unfold a certain way. I still tried to control outcomes. So, disappointments became opportunities to further surrender and have faith in myself and in Life. After several months of practice, I saw the magic more and more. I ended each week saying, "These amazing things happened this week. They came out of nowhere! I wonder what next week holds for me!" And better things showed up week after week. Money showed up unexpectedly, my husband got me flowers, a friend came for a last-minute lunch, business opportunities aligned, clients grew and ideas for this book presented themselves. I saw how much I continually received from Life on a regular basis. I saw how much I was supported by Life, just by allowing it to flow through me and for me. And the more I noticed these magical gifts, the more they came to me.

Today, I truly believe uncertainty means magic is about to happen. Uncertainty means the best is yet to come. Instead of fearing uncertainty, I now crave it. I consciously create space and uncertainty in my life. Crazy or genius? Probably a little bit of both. But think about it for a second: if you are comfortable with uncertainty ... more than that ... if you crave uncertainty, life becomes pretty fun, right?

In my first book, *The Self-Healing Spiral*, I talk about the three kinds of fear we experience as humans: the natural fear, the fear of the unknown and the fear of future possibilities. The first fear helps you step back when you are too close to the edge of a cliff. It helps you stay alive! We don't want to get rid of that one.

The second fear, the fear of the unknown or the fear of uncertainty, is what you experience when you are out of your comfort zone or taking a risk by facing something new or unexpected. This fear comes from the time when leaving our cave risked death. It was pretty dangerous out there! Wild animals could jump on you out of nowhere. Today, life is pretty safe out of the cave. There's no wild animal running down the streets, except maybe in Squamish where I live!

Yet, this second fear morphed into an overarching distaste for being out of our comfort zone. We fear taking risks, being out of control or doing something completely new. It's human and we will always have this fear. But studies show that the most successful people are the ones who feel this fear but take the leap anyway. Their ability to manage this fear makes them successful leaders.

The third fear is the fear of future possibilities. We create this fear when we consciously focus on the future and worry about all the potential worst-case scenarios. Some people experience this as constant worry or anxiety. Quite useless, this fear is also very unhealthy as it creates a lot of stress on the body. If you experience this fear, train your mind to come back to the present moment and remind yourself that you are safe, and all is well right now.

When you experience the fear of uncertainty, the second kind of fear, you have two choices. Perhaps you do something to try to make the discomfort of fear disappear. You fill in the empty space of your day with activities. You numb your fear with sports, tv, books, alcohol, sex, food. You come up with solutions. You analyze the best-case and worst-case scenarios. You push harder hoping things are going to work out. Maybe you even start worrying and fall into the trap of the fear of future possibilities. Or perhaps you do absolutely nothing about the fear but choose to feel it. You observe the fear that's trying to keep you safe. You feel it in your body, and you surrender. You accept. You stop resisting. You trust. You allow things to unfold. You acknowledge that you're not in control. You open yourself up to what is coming. You fill the space with silence. With intuition. With the present moment. And then, in the near future, something happens. Something happens because you allow Life, your co-creator, to step up. And your co-creator has way more power than you. And knows way better than you what's best. In divine timing, Life brings the next action or guides you toward it.

You must stop and surrender before you can take an aligned action because your mind has a limited perception of your reality. You perceive the future based on past events and how they unfolded for you. Like Dr. Joe Dispenza explains it, "We can't create a new future while we're living in our past. It's simply impossible." If you want a future that's different from your current reality, you need to change your way of thinking. But your mind only perceives 2 percent of your reality, which is basically nothing. So, even if you try thinking differently, you still deny yourself the full field of possibilities because you're limited to that 2 percent. You're so focused on what you want and how you believe it should come to you, that you can't notice other solutions and opportunities that are there.

Let's look at a concrete example. Look around and count all green elements nearby: a book, a plant, a glass, a piece of paper, a picture. Now, answer this question: How many blue items did you see? None, right? Your mind was so focused on green, believing it only needed green, that it didn't pay attention to anything blue. Long story short, when you operate from only your mind, you don't see other opportunities. You only focus on what you believe you need and overlook 98 percent of potential opportunities. So, let go of your mind. Let go of control. Surrender to the invisible, the greater, the co-creator—your intuition that guides you one step at the time and invites you to respond to your environment. Whether you want to win the lottery, meet your soulmate, buy your dream house or have a more successful business, your mind alone cannot comprehend how it could possibly happen. Use another strategy, the strategy of uncertainty. The strategy of surrender.

When you invite uncertainty into your life, you surrender to something bigger than yourself. You make space for something else to come through. You create moments to be filled with something though you don't yet know what it is. That's when you allow Source to work for you and through you. That's when unexpected ideas come, unexpected situations unfold. One minute at a time, one hour at the time, one step at the time, you move through your day guided by your intuition. You completely surrender to the present moment. You secretly and silently follow Source along the easiest path. You co-create your life instead of fully controlling it (not that you were actually really controlling anything since control is an illusion). If you accept and embrace this truth as soon as possible, you can co-create the amazing life you deserve. Of course, I am not saying everything is pre-written and you don't decide. You do decide. But those decisions are informed by Source, Life, the Universe, which brings signs, people, situations and opportunities for you to act on or not. You have free will and full power over deciding if and how you follow through. But the more you surrender, the more you attract opportunities. The more you let go of your resistance, the more you are positively surprised. When you move with the flow of life, the desires of your body, the nudges of your intuition, you open yourself to the field of possibilities. You access the magic of your highest potential. You allow the best to come.

At this point, you might resonate with the idea of surrender on a spiritual level, but your mind—your ego—is probably kicking and saying things like, "Yes, the best is yet to come, until it doesn't and something terrible happens." Or, "This might be the truth for you, but how do I know if this works for me too?" I get it. Shifting from the doing-mode to the surrendering-mode and hoping that life gets better is not an easy pill to swallow. After all, you've been pushing all your life and not always getting what you wanted. How could doing less bring you more?

I'm going to pamper your ego and your rational mind with four reasons why you are safe—right now, tomorrow and all the days to come. Allow yourself to see that the best is yet to come and that you can surrender to the magic of uncertainty.

1. *Where you are today is your worst-case scenario.* You have the wisdom, skills, creativity and resources to recreate your current life if anything happens in the future. You already got yourself here. You did it. You might have struggled along the way, but you learned so much already. You brought yourself here once, so you can do it again. Today is your worst-case scenario; tomorrow can only be better if you open yourself to surrendering and receiving more.

2. You manifested your current life with the thoughts and energy from your past. Because you are in constant evolution—growing, healing, reading this book, expanding and letting go of what doesn't serve you—your current thoughts and energy are higher than your past thoughts. So, your current energy being higher, your future can only be better! Your past energy manifested your current life, and your current energy will manifest a greater future! It's the natural process of life to always seek growth, evolution and expansion. Just like the trees that get bigger and taller year after year.

3. I assume that if you're reading this book and got this far, you are interested in healing yourself, peeling off the layers of your ego and unlocking your highest potential, right? Well, I have good news for you. As you heal and reconnect with your authentic self, you align with your soul more and more, and thus unlock future possibilities for yourself. The more you align, the easier life gets because life is supposed to be easy! It's supposed to be fun, experimental and joyful. Yes, we experience hardship, but only as growth opportunities, lessons, awakenings or realignments. We struggle because of our wounded egos. We hit walls because we are misaligned, and these walls bring us back into alignment. The more you heal your ego and align yourself, the brighter your future is because you further embody your soul. Your soul is naturally abundant, infinite and limitless, so your life becomes abundant, infinite and limitless. Isn't that amazing news?

These three statements, of course, only remain true if you regularly take care of your energy. Your natural state resonates with abundance, but your mind, traumas and worries disconnect you from this powerful vortex. The more you trust yourself, your skills and your wisdom and believe in yourself and in life, the more you access the truth of these three statements. So, take care of your energy, protect it, cleanse it and cherish it like it is gold. Of course, you can have days of grief and frustration. And you should. Feeling all your emotions allows them to flow through you and leave your physical and energetical body. But generally speaking, do your best to keep your energy—thoughts, mindset, emotions—high and surrender to whatever Life puts in your path.

4. One of the best ways to absorb a new belief is to base it on facts. You are safe and the best is yet to come but don't just take my word for it. Fact-check your own life, and the lives of others around you to help your subconscious mind shift to this new way of living.

Find proof that every time you thought about a worst-case scenario, it didn't happen. It turned out better than what you imagined. Go back in time and see how many stressful situations turned out well in the end. Maybe they didn't feel ok straight away, but in the end, the result was for the best. Journal on this for about 20 minutes to help your mind relax and understand that you were safe in the past, are safe in the present and will be safe in the future as well. More than safe, you will be amazed at what your life becomes.

When I think about the life I had three years ago, I would never have guessed I would be where I am today. As I write these words and look back to where I was, I am amazed. In February 2018, I was in India starting my spiritual journey. I was about to return to Belgium, to a man who wanted to divorce me even though we'd only married five months earlier. Before I went to India, I worked in a bank at a job that paid the rent but felt constrictive most of the time. I had a life that looked successful on the outside, but I felt like I was not really myself in front of my friends or family. I ate too much, drank too much and pleased others to cope with toxic relationships. Today, I'm writing these words on a sunny Friday afternoon. I started my day with a fresh morning walk under the blue sky. I'm inspired by this second book. I feel expansive when I work to help women and raise the consciousness of my community to make the world a better, happier, more joyful place one day at a time, one person at a time. I moved to Canada with its wild, stunning landscapes. I married my soulmate—a man so incredible that my wildest dreams couldn't even picture him. I'm pregnant with our first child, a boy that will bring us a lot of joy very soon. And we're buying a beautiful home that ticks all the boxes on my manifestation list. I'm still amazed at how Life guided us to this house. Never before have I been so comfortable in my body, loving my curves, my hair, my cheeky eyes. I have met new women who became like sisters and with whom I am completely myself, wild and authentic. I could go on and on about how much my life has changed. Was it easy? No. I had to heal myself. Stop myself. Let go of certain habits, people, behaviours. Learn to put myself first. Accept difficult truths. Be resilient in the experience of entrepreneurship. Was it flowy and an experience of surrender? Yes. All the inner work, the healing, energy upgrades and awakenings led me to create the life I always wanted. And on top of all that, I know the best is yet to come.

I know this in my bones because every time I faced uncertainty, every time I thought I was going to fail or needed money to survive, Life showed up and surprised me with something better. The worst-case scenario never happened. When I returned from my first Yoga Teacher Training in India three years ago, I had no money. I had spent all my savings on that trip. Suddenly, I had to face a divorce and all the costs that go with it. Two weeks later my employer paid my bonus and holiday pay money. It was enough to travel, attend another Yoga Teacher Training in New York City and pay for the divorce lawyer. A few months later, I quit my job and again had no savings. I wanted to move to Canada to study energy healing in Montreal. When I sold the flat I'd owned with my ex-husband, I obtained enough money to live on for 18 months, during which I invested in courses and retreats, traveled the world and launched a business. Unsurprisingly, my bank account ran low. But money showed up unexpectedly again. Over and over, things turned out better than I expected. Personally, professionally, financially. My new mantra became: "Everything will be alright. And if it's not alright, it's just not the end yet."

This is my experience with surrendering and trusting uncertainty. I hope that I showed you that if other people did it, you can do it too. Have a look back at your life and fact-check this for yourself to see how you're already supported by your co-creator. Then invite more uncertainty, more space, more surrender into your life. And if you're ready, here's how you can start surrendering today.

The Surrender Step-by-Step Guide

1. *Accept OR ask your question.*
   Acceptance is the first step of surrender. By accepting what is, you let go of the resistance you hold within. That resistance creates suffering. You believe things should be a certain way and because they aren't, it creates frustration, self-criticism and worry. Stop judging how things should be and simply allow them to be. By accepting reality, you open yourself to surrender and allow what's aligned to come through.

   If you need more support to accept what is, ask a question to your co-creator. Surrender is an experience of co-creation. Express your need for guidance or support. The more you communicate with the invisible world, the more it shows up for you. As with any relationship, start by asking your question or placing your request.

2. *Trust.*
   Trust yourself and trust Life. Behind all your questions lies the need to control. And behind the need to control lies the struggle to trust. You control everything because, deep down, you doubt that you can face a bad outcome. You doubt that you have the necessary resources to make things work. You doubt yourself. You actually do not trust yourself. It is difficult to face, and it broke my heart when I realized I didn't trust myself. But the sooner you recognize it, the sooner you'll transcend it. Once you see the truth of your own struggle to trust yourself, you see how resourceful you actually are. You rely on yourself. You trust yourself. And the more you trust yourself, the more you trust your co-creator, Life. This

external trust is only a reflection of your internal trust. But it is not something that happens overnight. It's built from small steps every day, tiny baby steps, until one day, you wake up and feel like you can really rely on yourself because you realize you actually already have everything you need within.

3. *Let go of your expectations and release attachment to the outcome.* Once you trust yourself, your resourcefulness, creativity and wisdom, you let go of your expectations. You detach from the outcome, the how and the when. Because your expectations come from your mind, they create two blockages.

First, expectations limit the field of possibilities. Because you're so focused on how things should be, you walk through life with blinders on. You can't see other opportunities; you can't see where Life wants to bring you because you're so convinced it should go a particular way. This 2 percent vision, again, limits you. It limits your capacity to receive a better, easier, greater plan, one that's waiting for you to grab because what is yours will always be yours. You are unique, and nobody can take away from you what is meant for you because it is simply not meant for them. So, let go of your expectations, broaden your mind, open yourself to possibilities and open yourself to receiving. You can repeat one of these two mantras:

- What is meant for me naturally comes to me.
- If it's not for me, something better will be.

Second, expectations lead to suffering. When things don't go the way you think they should, you resist them. You think, "It shouldn't have happened like this." "This person shouldn't behave like this." "Why is this happening to me?" "Things should go this way after all the work I've done on myself." You resist reality because of your expectations, and that creates suffering in your life, which, in turn, brings you back to step 1 and the need to accept what is.

4. *Create space in your days and in your body.*
   Space allows something new to show up. If your mind is too busy thinking, there's no room for new ideas. If your body is tense, there's no room for new energy to flow. If your schedule is tight, there's no room for something better to enter. Invite empty days. Long afternoons where you have nothing scheduled. Flowy hours where you just go with your gut, your intuition, the desires of your body. In that empty space, follow the joy, the fun, the flow, the movement of your day. Go inward and connect to your body; it will guide you on what to do next, what to listen to next, who to call next.

   As well as creating space in your days, create space in your body through movement. By moving your body, you move energy inside and create space within you to allow something new to come through. The energy of your life is a reflection of the energy of your body. As within, so without. Move your body to move your life. Go for a walk, move gently on the mat, dance and then sit in the space of your afternoon. Do something fun that your body wants you to do. Follow the nudges without any judgment of what you're doing. Be present to yourself without any expectation just by welcoming what Life offers you minute after minute. Savour your life ... and magic *will* happen!

5. *Receive and enjoy!*

This surrender process might look like a passive approach, a passive way of living, but actually it takes action to trust, to let go of expectations, to create space and be receptive. These are your actions to take, to surrender to Life and allow the best to come!

Trusting Oneself

Surrender has a lot to do with trust. You can't surrender fully if you can't trust. And I know from experience how challenging trust is. It's easy to say, "Trust yourself! Trust Life! Everything is going to be alright," but it sounds like a spiritual, useless cliche when you don't know what trust actually feels like. It is not easy to live in trust when you've experienced trauma, betrayal or abandonment. And we've all experienced that at a certain level. It's not easy to experience trust day after day if your experiences undermine it. It's not easy to know at your core that you're resourceful, safe and fully supported. If you struggle with this and experience more worry, anxiety or control than trust, then the next pages are for you. I healed my old control-freak-self to become a true surrenderer. So, I want to take you by the hand on this journey. And, trust me, it's a beautiful journey.

You experience trust when you feel safe. Your soul knows that you're safe, but your ego doesn't experience safety. Its main purpose is to keep you safe, so it constantly anticipates potential danger. It keeps trust at bay, so that it can do its job. It doesn't like safety and trust because if you lived in trust, then you wouldn't need your ego anymore. You wouldn't need his masks, tricks and control mechanisms. Your ego would slowly die if you experienced trust on a daily basis. And your ego doesn't want to die. It wants to live so that it can keep you safe. But not too safe! This curious paradox is why you never really experience trust. You're basically trapped in this paradox until you understand your ego's needs, heal him and give him another purpose, such as being a channel for your soul.

Some women, and I was definitely one of them, have a harder time trusting, whether it's themselves or others. Trust is one of the five main spiritual wounds we develop in childhood. Psychologist Lise Bourbeau explains in her book, *Heal Your Wounds and Find Your*

True Self, that children around five years old develop this wound when they feel betrayed by the parent of the opposite sex. It could be a very simple event where your father promises to take you to the fresh market on a Sunday for your favourite waffles. And on that day, he leaves in the morning to spend the day with his friends and comes back in the evening without saying a word. He obviously forgot the "promise" he made to you and probably also forgot he already had commitments for that day. Or maybe something important happened and he needed to leave. The reason doesn't really matter; it's how you perceive it that matters. It's how it makes you feel that matters. As a five-year-old, you're trying to understand the world around you, and you give meaning to everything. You wonder why your father let you down. You believe it's probably because of you. You believe you can't trust him, and he let you down because you are not trustworthy either. So, you stop trusting yourself. And as a result, you struggle to trust others. The way you trust others and Life is only a reflection of how much you actually trust yourself. To cope with this painful truth, your ego then creates a mask that you carry around for years until you choose to heal it. This is the mask of control.

You might wear this mask if you are super organized and love to plan everything. If you tend to be a bit bossy and show signs of confidence to the outside world. If you struggle to let go and are hard on yourself. If you're impatient and perhaps even intolerant. If you control others to manipulate them to behave a certain way. If you control a busy schedule, the food you eat, the way things unfold, chances are you have a betrayal wound and control is the coping mechanism your ego created because, deep down, you do not trust yourself. Acknowledging this wound is the first step of the healing process. Don't blame yourself if you recognize yourself here. We are all in this together. I used to be a real control freak, suffering from these trust issues. Daring to look at these wounds and love them without judgment helped me trust myself again.

Control is also a collective wound, coming from the wounded divine feminine, that society perpetuates. This leads us, women, to control when we feel unsafe or afraid. And this control impacts our personal, professional and intimate relationships, which makes things more complicated. Because who wants to be in a relationship that's controlled? Nobody. Especially not the controlling one. And we're all a bit controlling to a certain degree.

Control and trust issues not only impact your relationship to yourself and to others, but also impact your relationship with Life, your co-creator. You feel like you're the only one that makes things happen and you forget that you're a co-creator. But, when you trust and don't control, you actually co-create your reality with a greater force. An invisible life force makes things happen for you. Either you believe or you don't, but it is not something you can truly understand with your mind. The human mind wants proof; it wants to see before it can believe. That's its own way of controlling. But you feel it, understand it with your body, your heart, your womb. You understand it with the sensitive, subtle, intuitive part of yourself. And the more you understand that you're a co-creator and that this powerful other has a lot of gifts to give you, the more you trust. You expect good things. You see good surprises show up. You notice all the synchronicities. You observe the hidden hand behind it all. And you shift away from control and worry into trust and surrender.

Open your **workbook** (see Contents) to Exercise 11 and practice it to help you heal control and move into trust. For the next seven days, choose to apply this: Ex 11

Today, I choose to be patient and tolerant when something unexpected happens or when I wait for too long.

Write it down on a piece of paper, put it as a reminder on your phone, maybe even set it up as your phone wallpaper so that you can remember it and choose to practice patience and tolerance.

If you struggle with this, recognize that you gave your power to your ego, who convinced you that if you weren't controlling unexpected events, you were weak. Remind yourself that when you are more connected to your inner strength, you will not rely on external events to show you how strong and trustworthy you already are.

Healing Trust in the Physical Body

From an energetical perspective, trust finds its root in the first chakra, the root chakra. And from a physical perspective, trust is held in a very intimate part of your body, close to your root chakra: your yoni lips. They are the entrance of your sacred temple, your body. Trust is imprinted within your yoni lips. As is distrust. Every time you say "yes" when you mean "no," your yoni lips are imprinted with the energy of distrust. Whether you say a fake "yes" to please someone or to help someone out, your yoni lips energetically integrate that broken trust toward yourself. The imprint is even bigger when you have been forced to say "yes" and are a victim of sexual abuse.

Broken trust creates shame and triggers the whore wound and the collective wounded feminine addressed earlier in this book. You trusted your body by being flirty, sexual or self-touching and then you were shamed for it. Women have often been shamed for assuming their sexuality. Shame can also be self-induced. We are experts at beating ourselves up when we regret doing something, whether it's having sex or saying "yes" to something while we meant "no."

Trust yourself, your body, your "yes" and your "no" and don't shame yourself for your "yes" and your "no" whether it's related to projects, people or sexuality. By trusting yourself and your body, you change your relationship to yourself and to the world. Trust reconnects you with your self-confidence and power. You let go of shame, you let go of control and are able to fully surrender.

In your **workbook** (see Contents), spend some time contemplating and answering the following questions of Exercise 12. It's by doing the work that you'll experience breakthroughs, so get your journal and a pen and let the book open at this page. Make sure you allocate 15 to 30 minutes to answer these questions and allow insights to come through.

Ex 12

over

- When was the last time you experienced shame/beat yourself up? How do you feel now regarding this situation? What do you need to hear/tell yourself to let go of that shame?
- Why do you say "yes" when you want to say "no"? What fear makes you say "yes"? What do you need to do to trust yourself next time and speak your truth?
- How well do you know your "yes" and your "no" in your body? How do they feel physically? What differences do you notice?
- Energetically, how can you protect your own energy? How can you prevent others (their emotions, their worries, their judgment) from penetrating it? How good are you at holding boundaries? How can you only allow people to come into your energy when you are ready?

Your Biggest Takeaways from this Gift

....

....

....

....

....

....

....

....

....

....

....

....

....

....

One Action You Choose to Implement Today to Awaken this Gift

....

....

....

....

....

....

....

....

....

....

....

....

....

....

"*Change me Divine Beloved into One who can give and receive freely and be a clear vessel for Your Light.*"

—Tosha Silver

Chapter 10

The Gift of Receiving

Three Steps to Receive More of What You Want

When you receive a compliment, money or support, the flow of Life passes through you. You play a very important role in Life's natural flow. You enable the masculine, the giving energy, to do his work. Because the feminine receives and the masculine gives, both energies need to be honoured to allow Life to flow naturally. You are part of this cycle and if you give without receiving as much, you create an imbalance in the natural cycle of Life, which impacts both your life and the natural balance of Life itself.

When you want something, as a feminine being, put yourself in the receiver's seat and allow others—your clients, the Universe— to be the masculine giver. The feminine takes an indirect path, rather than a direct path, to get what she wants. She creates an environment that's favourable to receiving what she desires, instead of running after it. Concretely, that means you have to embrace the three spiritual laws of receiving:

- ◦ Ask and you shall receive.
- ◦ Release the "how"; it is not yours to figure out.
- ◦ You can only receive what you are ready for.

Start by connecting with your desires. Your deepest desires. And ask for what you want; express it to the right person or to the Universe, your co-creator. Then, let go of how it might possibly happen. Your mind cannot perceive how it might happen, otherwise you would have done it already. Sit back and allow what you desire to come to you in divine timing. Only take inspired action when it feels right. You will be guided. If you control and try to force things, you'll be in your masculine. Taking that role away from the Universe or your "giver" will transfer the feminine receiver role to your co-creator. This prevents you from receiving exactly what you want. Stay in your feminine energy and open yourself to receiving what you desire by behaving as if it was already there. That confident energy will show your co-creator that your desire is aligned with who you are.

This probably isn't what you've learned at school, right? Haven't you been told to push hard until you get what you want? You might even have learned to set SMART (specific, measurable, achievable, realistic and time-linked) objectives for yourself. It works, it's true. But only up to a certain point because it is a very masculine way of approaching life. And this over-achieving masculine way of doing things does not suit your receiving feminine energy. Rather than pushing to get what you want, your feminine energy makes it happen naturally. She asks for it, aligns her energy and opens her receiving channel in order to receive it. She lets it come to her by changing her energy.

Let's look at a concrete example. Social media makes you anxious and the screen time app lets you know that you spend an average of 3:06 hours per day on your phone, the average time American adults spend on their phones in 2020. You want to reduce your social media consumption. But how? You can set a time limit on your social media apps to force them to close automatically after one hour every day. You can delete the apps from your phone and only use them on your laptop. Or you can decide to go on a two-week social media detox. All of these are great masculine solutions to reach your goal. You are directly going for it. They could work, but they will come with frustration, struggle and tension because you are forcing a new habit.

The feminine path, however, is a path of ease. It is all about receiving and being indirect. So, rather than setting up strict rules to reach the new goal, you can explore how to effortlessly reduce your social media consumption. The reduction would be a side effect from this new environment rather than the direct goal. You can try to understand why you use social media and find that pleasure/benefit/satisfaction somewhere else. If you use social media because you're bored, give more time to your hobbies and passions or find a new hobby to automatically reduce your consumption. If you use it because you love connecting with people, set up in-person meetings around a coffee, a walk or a cooking class. If you go on social media because you're looking for social approval (likes, comments, shares), read a self-help book on self-confidence. By satisfying the need that causes you to pick up your phone and scroll for hours with another behaviour that is more fulfilling and healthier, you naturally reduce the time spent on your phone. You reach the goal indirectly by focusing on a healthy and fulfilling activity.

This example works for social media, but also for Netflix, binge eating, generating leads for your business, finding the love of your life, buying a house, making more money, etc. In order to receive, redirect your attention to other activities that make this happen naturally, effortlessly. These activities align your energy to that new behaviour. And it is that energetic alignment that allows you to receive the object of your desire.

Redirecting Your Focus

The receiving path is a path of ease, space and openness. If you want something to show up in your life, be an energetical match for it. Align energetically to that energy by focusing your attention on other activities that allow the object of your desire to unfold naturally. By changing your environment, belief system or habits to a new environment, belief system or habit where your desire naturally belongs, you magnetically call that desire and receive it in divine timing.

Redirecting your focus has everything to do with aligning with the vibration of your new identity. You behave as if it is already there. You make choices as if the object of your desire is already in your life. Simply by asking yourself, "How would I behave, what would I do, which choices would I make if I already had this," you answer the core need hiding behind your desire with other solutions. You then vibrate at a new level and energetically attract the object of your desire. That is the core of the feminine path.

So, spend time on activities that this version of you would enjoy. Change your habits to new ones that allow this desire to happen naturally. Redirect your thoughts to those you would have if you already had this thing in your life. Step into that version of yourself that has already reached the goal and change your beliefs, behaviours and environment accordingly. You are becoming an energetical match for this new goal of yours.

Creating Space

Whether it's physical, emotional, mental or energetical, you have to create space in order to receive. You can't receive a letter if your mailbox is completely full. You can't meet the love of your life if you're filled with anger and resentment toward your former lover. You can't have a friend sleep over if the guest room is filled with boxes, storage or books. Because we live in a world of energy, and because everything is connected, decluttering and physically creating space in your house could be all you need to do to receive new opportunities—business or personal.

When you create space by cleaning your house, releasing low vibrational emotions or throwing stuff away, you behave as if something new is about to arrive. You send a clear sign to the subtle world of energies: I am ready to receive, I am creating space for this.

A few weeks before starting to write this book, I felt a very deep longing for stillness. I felt that something wanted to come through, but I had no idea what it was. I needed to create space for this to birth. I decided to go on an information detox for six weeks. I stopped consuming all sorts of information in order to reconnect with my own intuition and creativity. I deleted all social media apps from my phone, dropped TV and limited my reading to one book. I had free time again, all throughout the day. During the second week, in the middle of a meditation, I suddenly had the idea of writing this book. My mind was still, so I could receive the download. I felt excited and joyful about the idea of writing on this passionating topic. I then waited a few days to see if I would receive signs confirming that this was the right next creative step for me. I received a very clear sign and then started writing. The creative process unfolded because I had created space for it.

So, whenever you want something or feel that something new wants to come through, create space in your life. Declutter your house, clear it energetically with sage, delete all sorts of mental distraction or heal emotional wounds through forgiveness and self-love. Then sit in that new empty space and allow it to come through. You needn't wait too long before seeing something happen!

Ex 13 Grab your **workbook** (see Contents) and open it to Exercise 13. Practice receiving your goals, instead of achieving them, through this fun three-step exercise:

- Identify what you want and why you want it. What is the core longing behind this desire?
- Let go of the "how" and redirect your focus: How would you behave if it was already there?
- Create space to receive: What behaviour/emotion/object do you need to let go to create space for this to happen?

Let's use examples to illustrate this magnetic way of receiving.

1. You want to participate in speaking gigs.
   - Why? Because you enjoy speaking and believe it's the best way to spread your work.
   - Redirect: You create short videos and post them weekly on YouTube.
   - Space: You let go of your writing blog.

2. You want to buy a bigger house.
   - Why? Because you're welcoming a new member to the family, and you need an extra room!
   - Redirect: You drive through the streets you like on your way home and visualize yourself parking in the driveway of the house you'd like to purchase.
   - Space: Discard all the clothes and objects you don't use.

3. You want to lose 10 pounds.
   - Why? Because you feel more beautiful and attractive at that weight.

- ◦ Redirect: Feel beautiful today and eat as someone who cares for herself.
- ◦ Space: Throw away the processed cookies, candies, ice creams.

4. You want to sign five new clients.
   - ◦ Why? Because you want to increase your income.
   - ◦ Redirect: Dress, behave and think as someone who is already overbooked and show up in the world with that energy.
   - ◦ Space: Let go of the limiting beliefs holding you back, such as "It is not possible," "I don't have a big enough audience," "There is not enough to go around," etc.

Saying "Thank You"

How comfortable are you when someone compliments you? How do you respond? I hope you say, "thank you." If you don't, I invite you to observe how you respond to compliments. Many of us deflect them; I definitely did. I remember a coaching client once said to me at the beginning of a call, "Oh, you look beautiful today." And I answered, "I wanted to cheer myself up this morning, so I put lipstick on." What a weird answer, right? Instead of simply saying "thank you," I felt the need to justify why I was wearing red lipstick. Did she ask why I was wearing lipstick? No. I answered a question she did not ask instead of simply saying "thank you" because the compliment took me by surprise. She politely smiled at my response, and, in that moment, I noticed I had rejected her kind words.

I did not honour her compliment by not saying "thank you." And when you do not honour what you receive, you are basically telling the Universe, "This is not for me." As a result, you receive less in the future. Because I am very well aware of this, I decided to open myself to receiving more compliments in order to receive more

THE PATH OF FEMINITY

abundance in my life. I said "thank you" more often to my husband when he complimented me. I bit my tongue when I noticed the old deflecting behaviour coming back and said "thank you" instead. It took practice to get comfortable with this new response. But soon enough, I found myself receiving compliments more and more. From the cashier at the supermarket, to the waiter at the restaurant, to the neighbour walking her dog, women took the time to tell me I looked beautiful. I would always stop, smile at them, honour their compliment and say, "Thank you so much." I am amazed at how often it happens since I began practicing receiving compliments and answering with a smile and a "thank you." Try it out for yourself, you'll see!

Japanese Zen millionaire, Ken Honda, conducted a study with 1200 self-made millionaires. He observed that most of them believe money is like air. It comes and goes like air. We breathe it in and breathe it out. He also observed that we receive as much money as we believe we deserve. The more you consider money from a place of abundance rather than scarcity, the more you open your receiving channel, and money flows in.

Mr. Honda teaches a simple method to attract more abundance into your life. Because money is energy, if you show signs of appreciation and gratitude toward that energy, you simply attract more of it into your life. By saying "thank you" to your money every time you spend it or receive it, you call in more of it. Instead of feeling guilt, wondering if you deserve it or struggling to press "pay," say "thank you," focus your energy on gratitude and heal your relationship with money one transaction at a time. This, in turn, invites more money in because it is a circular energy meant to flow through you and for you. Want to try it out?

THE GIFT OF RECEIVING

Your Biggest Takeaways from this Gift

....

....

....

....

....

....

....

....

One Action You Choose to Implement Today to Awaken this Gift

....

....

....

....

....

....

....

"A woman in flow of her Womb powers, through sexual Union, menstruation, or conception and birth, lives in a space between worlds, on the cusp of possibilities of both death and rebirth, a living paradox and chalice of life and dissolution."

–Seren and Azra Bertrand

Chapter 11

The Gift of Grounding

Womb Healing

On my spiritual journey, I discovered Light Language. I was fascinated by the healing ability of this mysterious language coming from the subtle realms and wanted to learn to channel it. As a musician, I loved the idea of adding healing sounds to my energy healing or coaching sessions. I signed up for a one-on-one course with a channeller and quickly learned to channel Light Language myself through drawings, dances, songs or spoken words. It was super empowering and completely out of this world at the same time. I loved it.

During one of our first sessions, my teacher said, "As I was channeling, a random download came through for you. You have to facilitate womb work and womb healing for women." Womb healing? I had no idea what that meant. I thought maybe it was linked to sexual trauma. Even though I have been through a lot of challenges in my life, I have been blessed enough not to experience this kind of trauma. In this life at least. I didn't understand how I could help women heal their womb and reconnect with that part of themselves having not been through such a healing process myself. It didn't resonate with me, so I left it there. When working with healers, psychics or mediums, it's always very important to stay in your truth. If anything does not resonate in the moment, drop it. You hold your own wisdom; others just give a message through the filter of their personality and interpretation. The same goes for this book—only take what resonates.

Three months later, as I was scrolling through social media, I discovered a coach, Lesha, who facilitates womb healing for women. I thought, "So, womb healing really is a thing. But what is it?" I read some of her posts, but they did not mention womb healing directly. I was a little confused and didn't give it any more thought. I moved on.

Another three months later, I was doing my Reiki master's degree with my friend Delphine. Delphine showed up in my life like an angel. We met in 2018 when I ordered a custom mala from her before I went to India. We connected instantly. Our relationship started as a healer-client relationship but quickly evolved into friendship as we began going for lunches together. We discovered that we have the same never-ending interest for spirituality. Today, we are like soul sisters and support each other with our unique gifts. At the end of this particular Reiki training, Delphine told me I had to look into womb healing. This was becoming a recurring theme! Thirty minutes after I left her house, she sent me a link to the Instagram account of Lesha, the coach I had discovered a few months earlier. How in the world did Delphine know her? The online space is filled with coaches, healers and therapists! The coincidence was too big. This time, I listened and reached out to Lesha without really knowing what I was getting myself into. I asked her if we could meet virtually, and she kindly agreed to tell me about her work. What started as a curious conversation ended with me signing up for an eight-week womb healing program. I had no idea what I was doing or why I was doing it. But my whole body was on fire when talking to her. I chose to trust myself and took the leap. It felt really scary—which, I know, is always a good sign.

As we worked through the seven gates of the womb, we released emotions, blockages and traumas that were stuck in my womb. I noticed changes in how I felt and saw how this work impacted my life's choices, my creativity, my intimacy and the connection to my divine feminine. It became very clear to me that I had to help women reconnect with their divine feminine. This womb healing reconnected me to my truth. I wasn't a victim of sexual trauma, but I was a victim of a patriarchy that had disconnected me from my power and my truth, and thus, my womb. It took me a few months to really understand that womb healing wasn't just womb healing. Yes, it is the emotional and physical healing of your womb space, but it is mostly a highly spiritual work that helps you reconnect with your power, creativity and divine purpose. Your womb is the source of your sovereignty, and through the healing of your womb space, you embody your divine feminine and create a life of purpose, alignment, success, wealth, ease and joy. It is now part of my soul's mission to guide you on this journey.

The energetical imprint of the wounded feminine has its roots in your womb. Through centuries of trauma, abuse and separation that women suffered, your womb space has become energetically empty. Your energy runs away from your three lower chakras, the seats of your grounding, power, creativity, sexuality and emotions, to find comfort in the upper four chakras. You disconnect yourself from your womb, making it harder to connect with your power and your soul when needed. This is particularly true if you have a career that serves others. Whether you're a yoga teacher, a coach, a healer, a therapist or you devote your time to helping others, you probably have a very heart-centred and intuitive approach to your work. This approach opens and develops the four upper chakras, but it keeps you even more disconnected from your power and the three lower chakras. As the consciousness of the collective also rises, and you choose the path of the heart rather than the path of the ego, your energy remains in the upper chakras, which hold part of your power back. That empty womb space combined with excessive energy in your upper chakras makes you anxious, and you overthink, overgive, struggle to feel your emotions, fail to bring your ideas into life, decline to speak your truth, repress your anger and boundaries and disengage from an empowered sexuality. All these can be healed by coming back in your body and in your womb. The wounded feminine leaves an empty space in your womb that needs to be reclaimed for you to reconnect with your power, your soul, your purpose and experience oneness with Source again. When you fully connect to your womb, you live a soul-led life. You become a creative channel of Life—knowing your power, living your purpose and bringing your gifts to Earth.

By healing your womb, you remember you are a vessel of the divine and embody this truth. Your womb is the centre from which you create—not only babies but also ideas and projects. Your womb is a physical place and an energetical place from which you create as the artist of your own life. It's a place where you are deeply connected to the infinity of the Universe. A portal to Source. A place where Life comes through. The energy flows from the Universe, top to bottom through you. You can also intentionally use this channel to connect to Source from bottom to top. It is in this flow of energy, coming through the sacred space of your womb, that you remember you are a vessel for Life. Allowing Source to come through you, to create through you and for you. It is in this space that you remember that you are Source itself—not just a drop from the ocean but the whole ocean in a drop, like the poet Rumi said.

It's time to take your power back after all these centuries of threat, deception, abuse and manipulation that you and your grand-mothers went through. It's time to water the bursts of creativity that grow like seeds in the ground, transform into tiny leaves and soon become trees creating oxygen for the whole Earth. You are the oxygen certain people need. And the secret of your unique oxygen, your unique purpose, is in your reclaimed womb.

Following is Exercise 14, which will help you restore the energy in your womb space. Grab your **workbook** (see Contents) and follow the detailed instructions: *Ex 14 one*

1. Sit down comfortably and place both hands on your belly, your womb.
2. Slow down your breathing—four seconds in, four seconds out.
3. Bring your breath into your womb and breathe like this until you find yourself feeling calm.
4. Visualize red feminine energy slowly coming up from the Earth into your left leg and filling your womb space.
5. Feel yourself sink as your womb is more and more nurtured by this feminine energy.
6. When you are settled, ask your womb:
   ○ What pain is ready to be released today?
   ○ What do you need?
   ○ What do I need?
   ○ How can I show up as my true, sovereign self today?
7. Allow sensations, images and words to bring you answers without trying to understand them straight away. You might need time to integrate the answer and be led to the right next step/action/self-care practice.

You can practice this exercise as often as you'd like. Additional womb healing exercises are included in the **workbook** (see Contents).

Grounding to Elevate Yourself

Pregnancy showed me how true it is that we are vessels for Life. A baby human grew inside of me day after day without any conscious effort from me. Yes, I had to initiate the process by making love with my husband, but the rest of it just unfolded naturally. And even though science explains very well that the meeting of a tiny sperm and egg is enough to create life and a sophisticated human body, I still cannot get my head around it. Being pregnant is more than just a normal event explained by science. It's a deeply spiritual experience that made me realize how much of a miracle we are. How much women are connected to the Source of all things, the source of Life. How much women are Life itself.

The gift of grounding invites every woman to come back to her body, her womb, the seat of her creativity and sovereignty. The seat of Life. The divine feminine is in her body. She dances, moves and seeks pleasure whether it is through the food she enjoys, the grass under her feet, the breath going through her lungs or the sun on her cheeks. She is very aware of what's happening in her body because she knows all the wisdom her body holds and has learned to listen to it. The divine feminine sees her body as the sacred temple that it is. It is the seat of her soul. The more she is in her body, the more she is grounded and present. She then allows her soul to be fully "em-bodied."

Grounding connects to the Earth, which is necessary to have spiritual experiences such as downloads, visions or kundalini awakenings. The spiritual journey is an inward experience that brings you to the centre of the Earth, the centre of yourself, the womb, the void, rather than an upper experience that connects you with the spirits above. Spiritual teachers often talk about opening the upper chakras, the third eye and the crown, to receive information and guidance from above. But if your first three chakra—those that help you stay grounded—are not turning properly, you won't experience a full awakening. The energy has to come down from the sky, reach the Earth and come back again in your body. If you're not grounded, the energy coming from above cannot settle and be received properly by the body.

The gift of grounding is probably the most important of all gifts because it allows creation. And you are here to create. It is the physical integration of everything you learn intellectually. There's no point in accumulating knowledge if you don't ground it into your life. It's why I share grounding last in this book; it truly invites you to bring everything from your brain to your heart to your womb. Bring it down from your head, through your whole body, into your life. From mind to matter. From the masculine, rational and logical, to the feminine, grounded and creative. The gift of grounding ultimately aligns you so that your soul can be fully embodied and lead you. Grounding allows your purpose to come through and enables you to automatically live a life of prosperity, ultimate health, blissful joy and constant flow.

Bring the following practices into your daily life to ground yourself and grow energetical roots from your subtle bodies—the seven spiritual bodies surrounding your physical body—into the Earth. To do these, first bring awareness to your feet, legs or first chakra. Remain present; don't be distracted by your to-do list, etc., or you'll lose all the benefits. After all, where your attention goes, energy flows.

- Walk barefoot in the grass or lay down fully on the grass.
- Go for a slow walk in the forest, and, if you'd like, hug trees.
- Massage your legs and feet in a warm bath with Epsom or Himalayan salt.
- Wear red pants or underwear, as red is the colour that nourishes your root chakra.

- Eat (spicy) food slowly to connect with your body.
- Dance to music with low drumming, or belly dance.
- Visualize roots coming down your root chakra and surrounding the centre of the Earth.
- Receive an energy healing session focused on grounding.
- Heal any kind of trauma that prevents you from being in your body.

Sensuality and Movement

The divine feminine is sensual. She uses her senses to be fully in her body—embodied. Your senses are the base of your sensuality. It is through feeling, smelling, tasting, hearing and seeing that you connect with your body and are ultimately led to your sovereignty. When you experience the world through your senses, you have a sensual experience and, eventually, a sexual experience because you create with your environment and sexual energy is creative energy.

Feminine sensuality has been shamed for centuries because it is a source of power. For a long time, I felt awkward when I saw videos of women dancing on social media. I always wondered why they would exhibit themselves like that. I didn't mind seeing them sing or speak, but dancing was too much for me. Even though I love to dance, and I am always the first one on the dance floor, I would never have allowed myself to post a dancing video on social media. Eventually, I understood my judgment was only a limitation of my own embodiment and power.

Movement is the true embodiment of the divine feminine. The feminine loves to dance. She loves to move. She uses movement to allow her feminine energy to flow through her, to express emotions, to connect deeper with the messages of her dreams, to connect with her truth, her womb, her power. Dance, yoga and silent walks are opportunities to tune in with your body and its messages. Were you ever surprised at feeling emotional on a yoga mat? Maybe even started to cry? It happened to me several times. My movement and position allowed stuck emotions to move, surface and be released. Movement is release. Movement is healing. Movement is connection to your sovereignty. Movement is sensual; you experience life through all your senses. Movement is sexual; it creates beauty. The more you move in a way that feels good and sensual, the more you awaken the divine feminine and can receive, surrender, be authentic, intuitive, magnetic and grounded.

How comfortable are you dancing alone at home?

How comfortable are you dancing with people around you?

How comfortable do you feel in your body when dancing?

Explore these questions and create more movement, more sensuality in your life to embody your divine feminine. Following are other ways to stimulate your senses:

- Slowly eat pleasurable, tasty food that smells good and is beautiful to see.
- Listen to music that pleases your ears and brings you joy.
- Wear clothing that feels soft and feminine on your skin and looks beautiful to your eyes.
- Feel feminine and beautiful with a simple beauty trick such as wearing red lipstick, a perfume that you love, putting on heels, long skirts, bangle bracelets, jewels or receiving a manicure.

Whatever you need to feel feminine and embodied helps you feel more connected to your body and in your sovereignty. Honour that beautiful body of yours. It is a temple.

Sacred Sexuality

We can't address the topic of grounding and the womb without talking about sexuality. Because sexual energy is creative energy, and your womb is the centre of your creativity, the more grounded you are and the more you connect to your body and your womb, the more you experience the sacred aspect of sexuality and creativity.

"Sexuality is sacred."

I heard this numerous times in my life. For me, it meant that you don't give your body to a stranger. That you create an intimate relationship with a lover first. It meant that sexuality is something unique. Not to rush, but to protect, to cherish and to choose with whom to share it. And all these things are true. But this is not what "sexuality is sacred" means.

One day, while having a very potent orgasm, I suddenly understood. I knew. And I'm choosing these two words—understanding and knowing—on purpose because my kundalini energy, also called sexual energy, reached my seventh chakra which is the seat of knowing and understanding all things. I suddenly knew this expression meant, "Sexuality is your most direct access to Source." This is why it is sacred. It connects you with the divine and is incredibly beautiful, powerful, pure, insightful and blissful at the same time.

When having this kind of orgasm, you feel a rush of energy go through your whole body, from your root chakra to your crown chakra. You might even have visions because the rush of energy sent through your chakras and sushumna, the energy channel in your spine, activates your third eye. You feel immensely powerful, limitless, expansive, loved, safe, wild. After the visions, you might receive downloads from a kundalini awakening. When this sexual, creative energy held in your root chakra travels your whole body and reaches your crown chakra, you experience a moment of enlightenment where you suddenly understand everything. Your mind is ultra active. You receive messages, insights and feel at one with the world. At one with Source. You know and experience the secret truth nobody told you about: Sexuality is your direct access to Source. In that very intimate moment, you realize that sexuality is a gift. It is the seat of your sovereignty and direct access to the whole Universe.

No wonder many religions consider sexuality sinful and shameful. We've been raised to see sex as disgusting, secret and not always pleasurable for women. There is a lot of mystery around sexuality in our Western world. We have definitely never been taught how to self-touch, self-pleasure or orgasm. Quite the opposite. We enter the sacred space of sexuality with a lot of vulnerability and no idea where our G-Spot is or how it functions. Women are called "whores" and shamed if too sexy. Some have their clitoris scarred to avoid any pleasure and some never have an orgasm. Imagine, instead, if we all accessed that power, that love, these downloads through sexuality, we'd realize how limitless and powerful we are. We'd be our own sovereign. We'd live in love rather than fear. We'd have fully embodied souls. We'd be unstoppable. Men, through the patriarchy, have long denied us that power in order to control us.

But this knowledge has been passed down secretly around fires, from one woman to another, in Mystery Schools or in Eastern countries. Mary Magdalene was initiated to sacred sexuality and practiced it with Jesus. She knew. Indians developed Tantra eons ago. They knew. Chinese Taoists also practice sacred sexuality to enhance their energy. They have known sacred sexuality for a very long time. And today, you know it too.

As a woman, you naturally have more feminine energy than

men. Generally speaking, as a feminine-essenced being, you are designed to receive—either the masculine energy from your partner or the intuitive insights. When you are in your receptive, feminine state, your intuition is fine-tuned. But you need to feel safe, appreciated and loved by your partner to fulfill this sacred experience. Only then can you let go of your barriers and enter a state of total openness so that your energy rushes from your root to your crown. If your chakras are aligned and your sushumna is clear, the kundalini energy rises up from the bottom of your spine to the top of your head. When it reaches your throat, you hear. At the third eye, you see. At the crown chakra, you know. Your clairaudience, clairvoyance, claircognizance and the other clairsenses are activated. More than your intuition, your higher senses suddenly turn on and you receive deep insights. Experiencing this blows your mind. You feel the rush of energy surging through your whole body, up and down and in circles, while you have visions and receive information coming from "nowhere."

You might wonder, "And what about men?" Well, men are mostly sleepy after ejaculation and don't really show signs of a kundalini awakening, right? There are a few reasons for it. First of all, men are in their penetrating, giving, masculine energy when orgasming. In that moment, they disconnect from their feminine intuitive, receptive energy that allows insights. They are less likely to experience that direct access to Source, unless they expect it to happen. They could consciously focus their energy toward the receptive energy of their partner to stimulate a kundalini awakening. When orgasming together, the energies of both partners flow between them and men can connect to the receptive, intuitive energy of the other. This would allow them to activate their clairsenses, receive insights and feel that instant connection to Source as well. Second, masculine energy has a different rhythm than feminine energy. It is less stable, more volatile and works in periods of rest and periods of intense activity. After making love to their partner, men need to rest. If they want to experience a kundalini awakening, they must consciously nest and connect with the energy of their partner. Finally, they must clear and align their chakras to experience a kundalini awakening and to connect with Source.

All individuals have feminine and masculine energy within themselves. Sacred sexuality is about how two energies relate and connect with each other so that the feminine receives and the masculine connects to her intuitive, receiving energy. What matters is with which energy you enter the space of sacred sexuality. If you are in your feminine, receiving state, you access this experience through surrendering, feeling safe and open. If you are in your masculine energy, and want to experience a kundalini awakening, consider connecting with the energy of your partner and focus your energy on receiving as well.

I address this topic from a place of personal experience and research, with the intention to uncover a taboo that shouldn't be a taboo. There is a lot of mystery, pain and distortion around sexuality, and it is difficult for most women to feel at ease in their sexuality. Who talks about this in Western culture? Did anyone teach you that sexuality is a direct access to Source? Do you realize that sexuality is a gift, a key? How comfortable are you in your own sexual life? How uncomfortable are you after reading these few pages? I choose to open this conversation because I believe it is important for us women. But I understand it is a tricky subject and I do not hold all the answers. I invite you to connect more with your body, your womb, your own intimacy and be open to the idea that you can experience what I mean by "sexuality is sacred." This openness and connection to your womb connects you with your sovereignty, your creativity and Source, in the sacred practice of sex but also in your entire life.

Your Biggest Takeaways from this Gift

....

....

....

....

....

....

....

....

....

....

....

....

....

....

....

One Action You Choose to Implement Today to Awaken this Gift

....

....

....

....

....

....

....

....

....

....

....

....

....

....

....

"Wherever there is power within, the potency of your light cannot settle."

—Arouna Lipschitz

Chapter 12

You Are a Sovereign Being

Sovereignty versus Power

A sovereign being vibrates the potency of its light. I use the word "potency" instead of "power" on purpose because sovereignty is actually the opposite of power. You must understand this at an intellectual level but also at the physical and cellular levels. Start by asking yourself: Even though sovereignty is the most powerful state of being, what's the difference between being powerful and being sovereign?

The last 2000 to 3000 years were all about power. We lived in the age of Pisces, and, as astrology teaches, the shadow of this sign is all about power and control. As we finally moved into the age of Aquarius with the great conjunction of Jupiter and Saturn on the 21st of December 2020, we were invited to leave power behind and replace it with sovereignty. We were invited to replace masculinity with femininity, strength with compassion, individuality with community, reaction with action. We are still invited to do so, as this transition will take several decades to settle. The time is now.

The power we need to let go is the capacity to direct or influence the behaviour of others or the course of events. This version of power relates to authority, control and influence on others, ourselves and Life. We want to influence others in order to feel powerful. We want to control others to reach our goals. We want them to behave a certain way to meet our expectations. We compare ourselves to others. We want to be as good as, or even better than, others.

We exert power over others but also over ourselves. We nag ourselves: "How can I become better?" "How can I improve myself?" "How can I control myself?" "How can I do the 'right thing'?" "How can I have more?" Always more. More strength, more wisdom, more wealth, more peace. The external power we exhibit is only a reflection of our attitude toward ourselves. We need to change within and heal our inner world to allow the age of community and sovereignty to take place.

The energy of power also connects us to Mars, the God of War. As we move from power into sovereignty, we move from Mars to its opposite, Venus, the Goddess of Beauty and Femininity. This transition invites us to face challenges and obstacles with tenderness rather than strength, with the intelligence of the heart rather than the mind because sovereignty has a very feminine energy, whereas power has a very masculine energy.

Can you see how power is the opposite of sovereignty? Power also prevents you from being in your sovereignty. It keeps the potency of your light in the shadow. It holds your sovereignty back. Wherever there is power within, your sovereignty cannot settle. You need to be honest with yourself, choose to heal and allow your own light, your own magic, to come through.

True sovereignty comes from your connection with Source. If you think that it comes from you, you are acting with power again. Yes, it comes from within you but only because the connection with Source lies inside. Sovereignty does not come from your ego nor your personality. It comes from something much more subtle and eternal: the connection of your Soul to Source.

Through sovereignty, you embrace and live from your divine feminine because that's where your connection lies. The Gift of Intuition, coming from your divine feminine, is your connection to Source. Your sovereignty lies in that connection because that's when you allow Source to be in you, to flow through you, to act through you, to protect you. You live like a true vessel of light. You remember you are Source itself and you are guided by Source every step of the way. You say the right words someone needs to hear. You read a book you didn't even know you needed. You go to that networking event and meet someone that offers you a great opportunity. You go to that birthday party you hesitated to go to and meet your soulmate in the middle of the dance floor. You release attachment to expected behaviours of others. You allow them to be. You allow Life to flow. Sovereignty transforms you into a channel of Life, a holy vessel, the expression of your unique essence allowing Source to guide it and act through it.

While being the sovereign of your life invites you to stay in the frequency of love and acceptance, it also supports you to let go of every need to control, react, struggle or battle. You heal at a very deep level and in all areas of your life. Start with your relationship with yourself, then explore how sovereignty is present, or absent, in your relationships with others.

Open your **workbook** (see Contents) to Exercise 15 to shed a light Ex 15 on the power you exert over yourself. By bringing awareness to your inner world and letting go of the power you have over yourself, you nourish your connection with Source. You open yourself to receive more and allow Source to work through you and for you. During the next week, choose to consciously observe your thoughts and actions. Every evening, light a candle and journal on the following questions:

- Where did I judge myself today? How did I judge myself today?
- What did I blame myself for today? Or convince myself wasn't the "right thing" to do?
- Did I compare myself to someone else today? What judgment did I hold toward her/him and toward myself?
- What did I try to control today—my partner, the outcome of a project, my input into work, my food?
- How can I forgive myself for trying to exert power over myself or someone else and start over tomorrow?
- Which thoughts do I choose to replace this with tomorrow?
- How can I rely on my connection with Source and always act from a place of no judgment and lightness toward myself?

Sovereignty in Relationships

Relationships are great opportunities to explore how you move away from power and into sovereignty because they invite you to be yourself fully and allow others to be fully themselves as well whether their way of being resonates with you or not, pleases you or not, triggers you or not. You're invited to act from a nonjudgmental place because, deep down, you know that we are all a unique expression of Source. It is, of course, much easier said than done because our humanness makes us judge and react, instead of observing and allowing with detachment. But the path of sovereignty is a path of full responsibility for what you experience, feel, think and create. If others hurt, trigger or annoy you, something hasn't been addressed within yourself. You create that trigger within. You hold on to it by playing the victim, judging the other person's behaviour or expressing your dissatisfaction. You give your power, your sovereignty, away to the other person.

Relationships make you grow like nothing else because they act like mirrors. And they can be tremendously hard. Whatever you see in others, whatever triggers you in others, sheds light on yourself. Relationships show you who you are and where you need healing. While it is important to take full responsibility for what you experience by asking yourself why you are triggered and how you can change that, it is also important to recognize others' behaviours that are unhealthy and where you need to set emotional, physical or energetical boundaries.

We all blame, justify, use emotions or hard words to get what we want. It's a way of exercising power over others, controlling or influencing them. We're mostly unaware that we enter relationships with a need for power. Dr. Stephen Karpman, founder of the drama triangle, explains that this need for power fuels unhealthy relationships. We play either the role of the victim, the saviour or the persecutor to have power over another person. We have all played, or still play, one of these roles. We have learned from society, parents or friends to unconsciously endorse them. And because many families, friendships or professional relationships function like this, we don't even recognize them as unhealthy anymore. We are simply used to it.

You might naturally tend to play one of these roles, like the saviour for example, but also inhabit the two other roles in different circumstances. Often, it's the saviour that wants to end the unhealthy pattern. The savior is tired of helping others all the time and forgetting himself or herself in the process. Nonetheless, playing the savior is a way to exert power over others. I know it can be a hard pill to swallow but hold on with me for a second.

First, when you play the saviour and save the other person, the victim, from a bad situation—finding him/her a job, lending money, intervening in one of their relationships, boosting their confidence—you do that person a huge disservice. It might seem great: you helped that person, perhaps even changed the course of their life. But, in actuality, you took that experience away from them. You took their power away. You prevented them from learning from that experience and finding a solution on their own, which would have helped them build their self-confidence and connect with their inner power. It is through our experiences that we grow. It is through our experiences that we heal. And Life always throws at us the experiences we need to heal, grow and expand. If those initial challenges are taken away, they simply return later, possibly bigger, to ensure we face them. These obstacles help us become who we were always meant to be. These obstacles are gifts in disguise. They should never be taken away from us by someone who believes they know better than us how to handle them.

Second, when you play the saviour and put your life on hold for the victim, you also forget yourself. You put the other person's needs before yours. You give away your power to the victim; they exert power over you. On the surface, you take their power away by saving them. But, deep down, you also give away your power because, in that role, you forget yourself and what is right for you. You are so involved in the other person's situation that you lose yourself. You think you helped the other, you think you won, but you actually lost. You both lost. There is no winner in the drama triangle. Just the illusion of having power over another. So, if you are a saviour and tend to save others from their own mess, please, stop. Take your power back and let the victim deal with it. You can support the victim and empower him or her by asking: "What is it that you need?" "How can *you* change the situation?" "How would you like this situation to be and what is holding you back from doing it?"

And what if a saviour wants to save you, foisting upon you the role of the victim? You could be sharing about a personal situation and have a saviour-friend or relative intervene with all good intentions. There are always good intentions behind these dynamics, but that does not make it healthy and sustainable. Shut down this power exertion by saying, "Thank you for your offer of help, but this is not what I need. If you want to support me, you can help me with this/by doing that."

The saviour comes from the wounded feminine or the wounded masculine depending on the intention behind its action. If the saviour shows up because they need to be in control, feel unsafe if others don't do what they want, worries easily or is manipulative, then they come from your wounded feminine. If the saviour comes from a place of being overly protective, overly giving and forgetting themself, then they come from your wounded masculine.

Then, we have the victims. They use emotions, tears, despair and complaints to exercise power over others. Crying itself does not imply that someone is playing the victim. No. Crying is healing and necessary to release tension, hopes, disappointments and pain from the body. But if those tears are energetically signed with despair, complaints or the intention to draw attention, then it's a power grab. Victims are easily recognizable because they believe it is never their fault and that they don't do anything wrong. They take no responsibility for their actions or emotions.

When someone plays the role of the victim, they inevitably give the other person either the role of the saviour or the persecutor. They make the other person the saviour by crying, asking for help or disclaiming responsibility or understanding of the situation. They make the other person the persecutor by not taking responsibility for what they experience or by blaming the other person for everything that goes wrong, often saying, "You did this to me,"

"You hurt me" or "It's your fault." If this is you, take back your power. Remember, no one can ever make you feel a certain way. You are responsible for your own emotions.

The victim typically comes from the wounded feminine. They are needy, dependent, inauthentic and struggle to speak their truth and take responsibility. Playing the victim actually is an opportunity for healing and empowerment. If you notice someone playing a victim role, let them have that opportunity, but help them take responsibility. This is the best gift you could give them. If you play the victim, give yourself grace and compassion. You probably learned this behaviour from your own parents or environment. Ask yourself: "What do I need?" "How can I give myself that?" "How can I change things?" "How can I express myself more honestly?"

The persecutor is the third role in the drama triangle. They are the "perfect" embodiment of the wounded masculine. They gaslight, avoid deep conversation, control the feminine by telling her how to behave, abuse verbally or emotionally. In these behaviours, the persecutor finds power because they are disconnected from their own power. They have forgotten that their true sovereignty lies in active listening, compassion, observation, protection, tenderness and their role to help the feminine stay in alignment.

If you choose to react to the persecutor by justifying yourself, you inevitably take the role of the victim and give away your sovereignty. Instead, leave the power game by saying one of these two things:

1. "How would you do it?"
2. "Yes, you are right."

Asking the persecutor how they would do something destabilizes them and forces them to see the situation from another angle. Perhaps they'll think about solutions instead of judging you. With this question in your pocket, you leave the toxic pattern and allow the masculine to move from its wounded self to its healed self. If they answer the question, of course ... but you have no power over that.

If they don't answer the question or you feel like it's a futile exercise, simply allow it to be. Don't resist their perspective. Release attachment to what the wounded masculine thinks because it is only a reflection of its own inner world. It means nothing about who you are. Allow the criticism to wash over you. Act like a sieve. Don't try to make your point, to show your perspective, to justify yourself and your behaviour. This only feeds the persecutor's power and traps you in the victim role. You know who you are. You know your truth and that's all that matters. Something you can do is to tell the persecutor that they are right and that you will take their judgment into consideration. By saying so, you disarm them. You end the debate. You allow them to think they won because all they want is that power.

This might feel inauthentic to you, and you might not want to tell a persecutor that they are right, but it's the best way to leave the unhealthy dynamics and stay in your sovereignty. You cannot have an authentic relationship with someone that acts from the wounded masculine and is a persecutor. Responding with compassion and care to that kind of behaviour is not caring or loving to yourself. You can set up that energetical boundary of letting them believe they got what they wanted and let their gaslighting behaviour wash over you. Allow them to be who they want to be, knowing that they are doing the best they can with the programming, fears, beliefs and experiences they have been through. Nonetheless, if you conclude that who they are is not acceptable and the relationship creates too much suffering, you can leave the relationship and set up a physical boundary.

Your energy is your most precious currency; you should never allow anyone to diminish it with their persecuting energy. You hold your own truth, and you know, deep down, what you need to do to honour it and honour your own energy. Your truth is all that matters and knowing your truth is what sets you free.

How the Divine Feminine Triggers More Healing

The more you move away from your wounded feminine and act from your healed self—that is, the more you let go of control, neediness, emotional manipulation, and know your power, surrender, are compassionate, lean back to receive—the more you are in your sovereignty. But as you change and evolve, so does the world around you, especially your relationships. Your inner shift inevitably impacts the energetic exchange you have with others. Some might love to see you more in your sovereignty, while others might be triggered by it since it presents an opportunity for them to heal as well. Do not be surprised to see relationships evolve and more people be uncomfortable around you.

Because everything begins with the feminine—the yin comes before the yang, as the yang is birthed from the yin—the healing of the feminine leads to the healing of the wounded masculine. The wounded masculine cannot see its own healing opportunity without a trigger. And your healed self is that trigger for men and women who live in their wounded masculine. As a sovereign woman moving from a place of empowerment, grounding, creativity, compassion, calm and receptivity, you trigger those who have not healed their own divine masculine. And when it shows up, the wounded masculine gaslights, judges, controls by telling you how to behave, expresses violent anger and blackmails. In other words, the wounded masculine plays the persecutor role to exert power over you because it feels insecure and uncomfortable in front of your sovereignty.

But stay in your sovereignty and have compassion for the inner storm that the persecutor endures. Also, remind yourself that all the aggressiveness directed at you has nothing to do with you, but everything to do with how the other feels about himself/herself. You are a mirror that is painful to look at. The persecutor blames others when they have not learned how to embrace healing opportunities. That just is.

The path of healing and embodying my feminine deeply impacted my close relationships. This healing opportunity for myself and trigger for others showed up in my life as I was about to become a mother. I had been playing the mother role for many people in my life and it was time for me to learn to be a mother for myself, so that I could, in turn, be a mother for my child.

When my brother was born, I was six years old. I was so excited about his birth that I spent his first night with him and my mother at the hospital, even though my father and sister went home. For the next few years, I always wanted to carry him, feed him, hold him, take care of him. My mother called me "the little mother."

As a teenager, my best friend would call me "mother" as well. If my friends went out and drank too much alcohol, I took care of them when they got sick. I made sure they had all they needed to quickly recover.

I even mothered my own parents. I would ask questions, listen, support, and comfort my mother when she would cry after difficult family dinners, or encourage my dad in his projects. Mothering is what I did and how I knew to interact with others. I chose partners I could mother as well. This role I inhabited made me feel safe and useful. But it was also a way to exert power over others and be loved. It was a heavy role for me to carry, but it was actually unhealthy for everybody. And I was responsible for that.

I had to let go of the "mother role" to birth the real mother in me. I stopped playing the saviour and I stopped allowing others to trap me when they played the victim. I started with my family of origin: my mother, father, brother and sister. First, I questioned my relationship with my mother, as our roles felt reversed to me. I craved the nurturing motherly love I gave her but felt like I never received from her. Let me be very clear that I do not blame my mother for being who she is. I know she did the best she could. She just did not know how to behave any differently. After all, she played the role of the mother, the saviour, with her own mother. As did my grandmother with her mother. And they all played victims in other situations. It's transgenerational, and as a divine feminine healer, the need to break this cycle roared in my heart.

I moved away from this dynamic by doing shadow work, family constellations and womb healing, and by honouring my own needs, letting go of my expectations, accepting her for who she is, expressing what was right for me and staying in my power even when my whole family used victim tricks because that was all they knew. We had unconsciously been living in this drama triangle dynamic all our lives. We took turns playing each of the three roles, though we tended to play one more than the others. That was what my parents knew and passed on. We did not know how to behave in relationships other than by playing the saviour, the victim or the persecutor. I don't judge it. It just was. Like in many families, we were used to it. But, when someone tries to leave the triangle, it creates chaos before it creates reorganisation.

My parents, brother and sister felt lost and disoriented by my new behaviours. They said that they did not understand me. According to them, I was on the wrong path. And I'm sure that felt true. I left a wounded dynamic that had been very unhealthy for me, for all of us. No doubt, to them, it looked like I was on the wrong path. They perceived me honouring my needs as rejection and selfishness. I moved into sovereignty and let go of the power they had over me. I also released the power I tried to maintain over them when I played the saviour or believed they should behave a certain way. Because everyone reacted from a wounded place, my journey created a lot of chaos and misunderstandings.

My inner shift triggered the wounded masculine in my brother and father. It showed up through messages and emails of gaslighting, control, blackmail, aggression, judgment, etc. It was painful to feel such violent anger and aggression, but I knew that it came from the wounded masculine. Having that deeper understanding helped me stay in my sovereignty, my connection to Source, and express myself firmly but calmly. Eventually, I allowed it to be without giving it my power, instead giving myself what I needed and staying in my truth. A new balance occurred, though they might never understand what really happened under the surface.

I share this very personal and vulnerable story because I want it to serve you. So many women feel stuck in their relationships with their parents or siblings. We believe family should be the cradle of love, the root of compassion and acceptance, but, in reality, family is often the root of transformation, and thus, the root of pain. Our families carry unhealed ancestral trauma because of centuries of power and patriarchal abuse. If you're reading this book and got to this story, you're probably the healer of your family. The black sheep. The one that does things differently and wants harmony in her life. But harmony does not necessarily mean peace in your relationships. Not yet at least. Chaos and pain often come before love and acceptance find their place. Rather, harmony is being at peace with who you are, honouring yourself and knowing why you disrupt the status quo. Harmony comes from respecting yourself and allowing your vulnerability to become your strength.

Moving toward acceptance helps you stay in your sovereignty during times of conflict. When you stop resisting the other person's behaviour, you stay in your sovereign power. Resistance creates suffering; when you resist something, it persists. It grows within you because, by not accepting it, you give it your power, your sovereignty. When someone does or says something that does not feel right, don't hold on to it. Allow it to be. Let go of the belief that he or she should have behaved differently, lest you attempt to exert control and power over them. People do the best they can. If they knew how to behave differently, they would. You needn't ignore or overlook their attitude, but you have to accept it. Take note of their behaviours, words and actions and integrate it as who they are. Then choose if this is aligned for you or not. Decide whether the energetic exchange of the relationship suits you. Observe how you feel when you are around them and question if it is an opportunity for growth, healing or setting a boundary. If their attitude simply does not suit you because it clashes with your values, accept it and set energetic boundaries by allowing the other to be who they are but give less of your time and energy to the relationship. Being a sovereign in relationships balances accepting the other person and choosing how much of your energy feels right to invest in the relationship. You don't have to justify or explain that amount. But, as you're the only one who knows what you need, you're responsible for deciding and implementing those boundaries.

To stay in your truth and not fall into the victim trap, remember why you trigger people and why they criticize or gaslight you. It has nothing to do with you. Your existence simply reveals things about themselves that they don't want to face. There are four reasons that people judge.

1. *Mirroring: We see our own weaknesses or faults in the other person.*
    Ex: A bossy person struggles with authority and criticizes

someone who's controlling. Very often, when people criticize you, they judge a part of themselves they see in you. They call you out for being a certain way, but actually act that same way themselves. In your sovereignty, you realize the criticism does not apply to you; you simply mirror their weakness. You actually help them see more of themselves.

2. *Projection: We project unfinished relationships (parents, siblings, ex-partners).*
   Ex: Your ex-partner has ended the relationship by blaming you for its demise and did not respect you in the ending of the relationship. As a result, you might feel rejected and not good enough, but you did not express it. If someone else treats you in a similar way, you could suddenly release all your anger, frustration and pain on that second person. In reality, this emotion is a byproduct of the unfinished relationship related to the first person.

3. *Restriction: The other person does something we do not allow ourselves to do.*
   Ex: Others play theatre and act extravagant on stage, wear miniskirts or travel the world. Do you criticize others for doing something you actually crave but deny yourself? Do you tend to qualify things as good or bad, right or wrong? If so, you limit yourself with these judgments. Seeing others do some thing you desire is an opportunity for you to let go of your judgment and permit yourself to go after that activity/dream/project/behaviour.

4. *Values: We have different values and act differently based on these values.*
   Ex: If you value freedom, a person who lets themselves be restricted triggers you. If you value generosity, a selfish person triggers you. Knowing that our egos choose these values to

keep us safe helps us accept another person's values. They are simply different; there are no values better than others. I encourage you to identify your values by brainstorming, taking an online test, etc., so that you can easily recognize when some one has values opposite yours.

Every single trigger is an opportunity for you to grow, discover yourself more deeply, heal and let go of limiting beliefs. With these four points in mind, whenever a person triggers you, ask yourself:

- Why does this trigger me? Do I also carry this personality trait?
- Did someone treat me in a similar way recently? Does this person's behaviour remind me of someone in my close circle? What did I not express to the first person?
- Is this person doing something I would really like to do but deny myself?
- What are my core values? How could this behaviour be opposed to my personal values?

People judge and criticize when triggered by you because you reveal an opportunity to heal, which feels uncomfortable, if not painful, to them. This is your opportunity to stay in your truth, in your sovereignty and let that judgment wash over you. Like my teacher Makhosi always says: "Be a sieve."

Devotion to Your Sovereignty

You are on a path of healing. It's a journey that brings you all around your inner world. From the deep blue oceans of your emotions to the snowstorms of your mind to the relaxing lavender fields of heart. You might want to quit certain days, and that's alright. You can always return to this path of self-devotion. Day after day, trigger after trigger, fear after fear, you are invited to come back to loving yourself and bathing in your connection to Source, in your heart, in your womb. The path of Sovereignty invites you to awaken your six hidden natural gifts so that you can embody your divine feminine fully and experience more alignment, wealth, joy, freedom, ease, intuition and expansion. This becomes your new normal:

- Authenticity. You are fully yourself. Fully unique. Allowing yourself to be seen for who you are. Allowing your light to shine. Sharing your unique gifts. Speaking your unique truth. Holding nothing back, especially not what you once considered too much or shameful. This too-muchness is your authenticity, your uniqueness and other people need it. You also put yourself first, knowing this is how you recharge your authentic energy to give your ultimate best to others.

- Magnetism. You are full of yourself. Knowing you do not need others, their approval, their support or their love to be full. You are a complete, whole being. You find happiness and fulfillment within yourself and within your connection to Source. You do things slowly, with care and allow divine timing to unfold. And that makes you terribly magnetic. You naturally attract the right people and opportunities to create the life you have always dreamt of.

- Intuition. You are full of wisdom and creativity. Allowing your sensory receptors to receive and transmit new and unique information as you connect with your higher self and the subtle realms. That intuition guides you and you respond to it. You are a vessel for Life.

- Surrender. You are full of trust. Letting go completely and handing the last bit of your power to the co-creator of your life. Knowing everything always happens in divine timing as you actually have no control or power over people or things. You know everything is always perfect even if it might not look like it.

○ Receiving. You are full of life, as you allow Life to come through you. You receive all of the time. And the more you reconnect with the abundant Source that you are, the more that abundance reaches you and flows through you. When you receive, someone else gives. You allow the infinite circle of Life to flow. You live in gratitude.

○ Grounding. You are fully embodied. Your light, your soul acts through your body, which is a pure channel for your soul to do its work. The more you are in your body— moving it, consciously feeding it, choosing with it, deciding from it—the more grounded you are. And the more grounded, the more you reach the sky and access deeper intuition. Ultimately, you connect to your womb and know your sovereignty and connection to Source lies in there.

Working through each of these six gifts individually is a great way to reach sovereignty. The previous chapters offered hands-on tips and exercises for you to start healing and awakening these feminine gifts. You can also address them by choosing to let go of your power. This slowly and naturally unlocks these gifts. Relying on your connection with Source is a journey in itself. Don't judge yourself on this path but welcome the growth and the integration of more of yourself. Let go of the power you have over yourself, and you inevitably release the power you attempt to exert over your connection with Source, and thus enable more of it to come through.

If you find yourself in a situation that challenges your sovereignty, where the powerful being you were before is triggered, recognize the behaviour, words or attitude of the other person. Accept them for what they are and allow them to be with detachment. Then choose if being around this person is aligned with your values or your highest good. If it's not, then detach from the expectation that you can change the other person to make him or her behave a certain way. Allow the other person to be and explore the journey of sovereignty on its own timing. Take care of the potential emotions if this interaction awakens something in you. Finally, focus your time and energy on yourself and be grateful for the teachings offered in this interaction.

Last but not least, true sovereignty happens through embodiment. And by embodiment, I mean leading by example. The more you live in sovereignty, the more you inspire others to do the same. And that's how we shift the consciousness of humanity, one person at the time. Children learn from our actions, not from our words. Adults aren't any different. We are inspired by people's actions, rather than their words. We observe their attitude more than we listen to their words. If you want to be a feminine leader and play your part in the rise of the divine feminine on Earth, be a true embodiment of your own sovereignty. Be a true embodiment of these six gifts. It is the greatest gift you can give yourself and give humanity. Teach others how to get there by being authentic in your vulnerability, creativity, groundedness and receptivity, rather than by telling them how to behave. Though I write this for you, it also serves as my everyday reminder that we teach by who we are, rather than what we say. Let's be the change we have been waiting for.

Your Biggest Takeaways from this Chapter

....

....

....

....

....

....

....

....

....

....

....

....

....

....

One Action You Choose to Implement Today
to Develop Your Sovereignty

....

....

....

....

....

....

....

....

....

....

....

....

....

....

"*The world changes when we change. The world softens when we soften. The world loves us when we choose to love the world.*"

—*Marianne Williamson*

A Note from Me to You

We live in a world of power. A world where money, power and status are praised and sought, consciously or unconsciously. We are shown through movies, social media and the press that the more money, power and status we have, the more respected we are. Is this the best way to be?

It doesn't have to be like this. It doesn't have to stay like this. And I honestly, truly believe it starts with all of us women. We *can* change society into a world where authenticity, acceptance, community and care are at the centre of our exchanges.

We, women, have the key to create it, because we are the creators of the world. We are the birthers of tomorrow's leaders, influencers, creatives and inventors. If we heal ourselves, heal our wombs of all the ancestral trauma that led to the world we live in today, and come back to our sovereignty, remembering that we are divine and that all of it starts in our wombs, we will lead a new humanity. We will birth a new humanity.

I know it sounds cheesy and idealist, but I truly believe this to be true. We all come from wounded families that have been through horrendous experiences, but if we can heal, forgive, have compassion and choose to start over with our own families, with ourselves, with bringing our feminine power to the world through our businesses and lives, we will give life to a New Earth.

And it starts with you. The woman that you are. The mother you are or will be. The leader you embody. The friend you show up as. The business you run. Your presence makes a difference. You make a difference just by being fully you.

Now that you've read this book, I invite you to devote yourself to your sovereignty. Devote yourself to living in feminine flow. Devote yourself to embodying your soul's purpose in your business and creating a life that feels aligned, joyful and playful. Life is not supposed to be hard; it is a playground where we birth the ideas, families and businesses that bring us the most joy. That's what you came here to do. That's why you're here. That's why this book ended up in your hands.

Create your playground, dear divine feminine. And let's change the world together.

About the Author

Eléonore de Posson is a spiritual teacher and visionary for the New Earth. She helps women run their businesses and lives from their feminine energy so that they can magnetize more magic and wealth. Using her gifts of depth, wisdom, practical leadership and healing, Eléonore empowers women and helps them heal, have a soul-led life and serve humanity with their own gifts. She is also the author of *The Self-Healing Spiral*™ and host of The Sacred Roots Podcast.

www.eleonoredeposson.com

@eledeposson

The Sacred Roots Podcast